# A Good Life

Sally Rynveld and Guy Winship

# A Good Life

The story of Guy Winship and Good Return

The authors are grateful to Arundhati Roy and David Godwin Associates for permission to reproduce a quotation from her article 'The end of imagination', first published in *The Guardian* on 1 August 1998.

The authors are grateful to Regal Hoffmann & Associates and Pan Macmillan Australia for permission to reproduce a quotation from *Shantaram* by Gregory David Roberts. Copyright © Gregory David Roberts 2003.

The authors are grateful to the Philosophical Library Inc. for permission to refer to a quotation by Jean-Paul Sartre from *Existentialism and Human Emotions*, first published by Citadel in 1957.

*A Good Life: The Story of Guy Winship and Good Return*
ISBN 978 1 76041 583 9
Copyright © Sally Rynveld and Guy Winship 2018

First published 2018 by
**GINNINDERRA PRESS**
PO Box 3461 Port Adelaide 5015
www.ginninderrapress.com.au

# Contents

| | | |
|---|---|---|
| Foreword | | 9 |
| Prologue | | 13 |
| 1 | The early years | 17 |
| 2 | A developing consciousness | 34 |
| 3 | Love and loss | 47 |
| 4 | 'Toilet Guy!' | 64 |
| 5 | 'Rats ate my money!' | 84 |
| 6 | Starting over | 101 |
| 7 | The nuts and bolts of microfinance | 116 |
| 8 | Making it happen | 135 |
| 9 | In the field | 148 |
| 10 | The birth of Good Return | 164 |
| 11 | Facing the bully | 191 |
| 12 | What is a good life? | 205 |
| Afterword | | 215 |
| Acknowledgements | | 217 |

To my immediate and very precious family: my wife, Jacqui and my two children, Thomas and Brontë. Thank you for all your love and support. I am extraordinarily lucky to have the three of you in my life.

And to the hundreds of thousands of vulnerable women who Good Return has worked with and supported, directly and indirectly, over the years: thank you for making me a better human being.

Guy Winship, January 2018

The only dream worth having…is to dream that you will live while you are alive and die only when you are dead… To love, to be loved. To never forget your own insignificance. To never get used to the unspeakable violence and vulgar disparity of life around you. To seek joy in the saddest places… To respect strength, never power. Above all, to watch. To try and understand. To never look away. And never, never to forget.

Arundhati Roy

# Foreword

Guy Winship stumbled into my life in August 2003. Literally. Flustered from having just lost his passport, Guy arrived late at the Australian Embassy in Beijing, where I was working on Australia's aid program in China. We were due to spend the next two weeks in western China, evaluating a microfinance program. Little did I know then that Guy would become a mentor and dear friend, and that those two weeks would turn into fifteen years.

The first things that struck me about Guy were his energy and gregariousness. He engaged eagerly with everyone he met, regaling them with stories and jokes before interrogating them about their life and work. Whether dealing with a government official or a poor villager, Guy's genial and disarming manner, and his genuine interest in people, quickly put them at ease and got them to open up.

Over the next two weeks, I discovered in Guy an astute professional, knowledgeable about all aspects of microfinance and passionate about its ability to change lives. It was hard not to be swept along by Guy's optimism and zest for life. I had a great time over those two weeks; our days were filled with stimulating conversation, laughter, thoughtful reflection and meaningful work. At the end of the trip, when Guy asked me to join him in his fledgling organisation, my answer was never really in doubt.

Guy thrives on a challenge: moving to a new country and setting up what was to become a highly successful charity were nothing short of extraordinary. It is testament to Guy's strong sense of community and social purpose that he chose to set up a non-profit organisation rather than a commercial consulting business. In the early years, Guy generated significant consulting income, but it all went into growing

Good Return. Not only did he forego that additional income, but as the organisation experienced inevitable growing pains over the years ahead, he dipped into his family finances to ensure that staff were paid on time, every month. In addition to putting in the long hours and carrying the burden of responsibility, Guy put his money where his mouth was, being one of the organisation's primary donors over many years. As a result of Guy's effort and initiative, Good Return grew from a fledgling organisation to one that has benefited the lives of hundreds of thousands of people across Asia and the Pacific.

The team at Good Return have a deep and enduring affection for Guy, and news of his cancer shocked and saddened everyone. But Guy wears his heart on his sleeve and, with his wit and sense of humour, he can lighten any situation. After having his eye removed and getting fitted with an artificial eye, we waited expectantly at the office to see how the new eye would look. Guy walked in with one eye closed, then grinned and opened his eyelid to reveal a white ball with 'Good Return' printed on it, in the organisation's trademark colours. To add to the joke, he announced, quoting Erasmus, 'In the land of the blind, the one-eyed man is king!'

Considerate and generous, Guy has won friends wherever he has ventured. Those who get to know him well invariably develop a deep fondness for him, and even when they move out of his immediate orbit – whether as an employee, director, colleague, squash partner or friend – they tend to stay in touch. As a result, some have likened Good Return and their acquaintance with Guy to the Hotel California: you can check out any time you like, but you can never leave. I would extend this sentiment to Guy himself.

Guy has done more than cast a stone into the waters of international development work: he has made a big splash, and the waves will continue to ripple far into the future, inspiring others to keep striving to make this world a better place.

Shane Nichols, CEO Good Return

# Prologue

A young soldier crouches on the ground below a canopy of branches. His forehead and upper lip glisten with sweat. All around him is dense scrubby bush. The air pulses with heat. Beside him stands a field mortar: a tube, sixty millimetres in diameter and about two-thirds of a metre long. Fifty metres ahead, there's a short burst of gunfire, followed by another from further away. The men from his platoon start shouting at him to fire the mortar. He tries to see what's ahead but he can see nothing through the jungle. They're yelling at him to aim the mortar two hundred metres ahead of them. More gunfire. More shouting. He has to move fast. Hands shaking, slippery with sweat. Heart thumping. Mind numb with terror. He tries to think straight, to work out the angle of the trajectory, aim the mortar right. He lifts the bomb, drops it into the black barrel of the mortar.

The bomb travels a short distance before hitting a tree and exploding less than thirty metres away. Huge clouds of smoke billow everywhere. Dazed, the young soldier realises his mistake. The bomb he loaded into the mortar was a smoke bomb, not a half-kilogram of high explosive.

It was a mistake that saved Guy Winship's life.

We were in what was called a fire fight: a fleeting confrontation. We were under a tree, with branches above us. Not a place you want to be as a 'mortar guy', because a mortar fires up at an angle and the bomb goes miles into the air. But in the heat of the moment you can't stay focused all the time. Sure as nuts, if I'd loaded the mortar correctly with a high explosive instead of a smoke bomb, I'd be dead.

Guy had been in the army for about five months when this incident happened. He was just nineteen. After a few weeks' training as a mortar operator, he'd been helicoptered into Angola to fight a war he knew almost nothing about.

All I take from this incident, this war, fighting in dense bush in the middle of nowhere, is shame and regret. There weren't any victors. How would a German soldier have felt at the end of the Second World War? I guess that's how I felt. Even if we'd won the battle, we lost the war.

But there's something else. When I think back to that time, it's as though, at the age of nineteen, I was given another chance. From nineteen until now, aged fifty-five, I've been given all that time. What matters is what I've chosen to do with that time. That's what matters to us all.

∞

I first met Guy thirty-five years later, when we were both working on a rural development project in Sri Lanka. He had already been travelling around Sri Lanka for about ten days and was due to return to Australia that night.

I was looking forward to meeting Guy. I'd been told by a colleague to expect a pleasant, congenial bloke with impressive credentials. We had arranged to meet in the vast marble and chrome lobby of the Cinnamon Grand Hotel in downtown Colombo.

Striding across the hotel lobby, he approached me with a big grin and a look of eager expectation. He shook my hand vigorously. 'Let me tell you about what I've been doing,' he began. 'How long have you got?'

I'd expected a short meet-and-greet, but Guy steered me towards the café adjacent to the lobby and launched into the fundamentals of microfinance. Within an hour, he had convinced me that microfinance – specifically village-based savings and loans – wasn't simply an important element in this rural development project. For Guy, microfinance is not only about helping individuals and their families to lift themselves out of poverty; providing savings and loans services for the poor is an essential key to reducing poverty worldwide. What impressed me wasn't simply the extent of Guy's technical knowledge; I already knew he was an expert in his field. What really struck me was his energy and enthusiasm – his sheer passion for his work.

That first meeting was more than twelve years ago. In 2003, a few years earlier, Guy had established a microfinance non-government organisation (NGO) – World Education Australia, later to be known as Good Return. Starting out on his own, Guy quickly built the enterprise into a small team operating out of a tiny office in Chatswood, northern Sydney. Over the next fifteen years, the organisation evolved and grew to become a significant enterprise with a multimillion-dollar annual turnover, a high-flying board of directors and a team of more than sixty staff and volunteers working in Australia and overseas.

∞

In 2013, Guy was diagnosed with ocular melanoma – cancer of the eye. His left eye was surgically removed and he recovered fast. The prognosis was reasonably good. He threw himself back into his work with Good Return, and life returned to normal, more or less.

For about half of those diagnosed with ocular melanoma, removal of the affected eye is the end of the story. They recover completely. For the other half, however, the cancer spreads. It might take months to metastasise, or even years, but in all of these cases it's terminal. Without exception. A year after his initial diagnosis in November 2014, scans showed that the cancer had spread to his liver and his bones. He was told he had a year to live.

But more than two years later, Guy was still working as hard as ever. In early 2017, he and I got together one Saturday morning for a late breakfast at a crowded café in a busy Sydney shopping centre. It had been at least six months since we'd last met; we had a lot of catching up to do. After ordering our second cappuccinos, I asked Guy whether he'd considered writing a book about his life.

'Yeah, I've thought about it,' he said, 'but I've got to admit I'm no writer.' He'd been approached by a few journalists who were interested in his story, but he wasn't comfortable with the idea of talking openly to strangers.

I took the plunge and proposed that he and I might write his story together, perhaps as a series of conversations. Guy's response was immediately positive. I felt at once thrilled and privileged, and – although it sounds corny – I felt honoured. And not a little anxious. It was a daunting prospect, particularly given the state of Guy's health. We couldn't waste time.

As Guy put it, 'If I'm ever going to do this, I need to do it now.'

Our first conversation took place four weeks later on a muggy autumn morning at Guy's home in Belrose, Sydney. We sat out on the deck at the back of his house surrounded by lush, subtropical greenery, masses of shrubs and large tubs of white, pink and yellow flowers: 'Jacqui's garden', Guy calls it – Jacqui being Guy's wife of the last twenty-five years. The sky was deeply overcast, the light subdued and almost gloomy. It was very humid, with the promise of rain any minute. As we talked, the mood – like the sky – shifted from light to sombre and back to light as Guy moved from one anecdote to another.

His natural ebullience and humour were never far from the surface: 'You've got to keep your sense of humour!' he would chuckle, and then he'd erupt into laughter. It was quite surreal.

Guy talked about his family, about his early awakenings to the inequalities and injustices of life in South Africa, and of his two years of compulsory military service when he was in his late teens. He reminisced about teaching Dickens to kids in a black township on the outskirts of Durban, about joining the African National Congress and his contribution to their work in the lead-up to the first democratic elections in 1994, and about how he refused to serve his final two years of military service – a decision that proved seminal in influencing the direction his life would take. He talked about working with the poor, about microfinance, about development, and about Good Return, the organisation he had created fifteen years earlier.

With characteristic directness, Guy also talked frankly about his disease and prognosis. 'The truth is a bully we all pretend to like,' he observed, quoting from *Shantaram*, one of his favourite recent reads.

The truth, in this context, was of course the fact that his cancer is terminal. Although he is uncertain what he believes spiritually, Guy confronts his own mortality with honesty and courage.

Our first conversation did more than set the scene for his life story: it confronted, head on, the reason why writing his story was so important and so urgent.

# 1

# The early years

'I never let schooling interfere with my education' – Mark Twain

I was born on 6 September 1961 in Durban, South Africa, into a life of comfortable, middle-class privilege. If I'd been born a girl, I was going to be called Victoria, but I turned out to be another boy – hence the name 'Guy'! My two brothers, Mark and Jonathan, and I were all born by Caesarean section. My mother had a few miscarriages in between Mark's birth in 1956 and my arrival in 1961, and then Jonathan was born three years later. I think my parents would have liked to have had a girl, but after three Caesareans the doctor said, 'No more!'

My earliest memory is from my third birthday. I remember blowing out the candles on my birthday cake, then afterwards sitting on the steps from the veranda – they call it a stoep or porch in South Africa – down to ground level at the front of our house in Durban. Sitting there on the stoep with my family, watching friends leave.

My brothers and I had a lovely, easy upbringing. We were pretty well-off, I guess; we lived in a large house opposite a park in an all-white neighbourhood. We had servants: a maid, a gardener, and a nanny when I was young. I just took these things for granted, then; I suppose we all did, all of us kids. The family would eat in the dining room every evening, with my mother at one end of the table and my father at the other. Mom would press a buzzer under the table with her foot, and out would come the maid with the first course. Then Mom would press the buzzer again, the dishes would be cleared, and we'd get served the main course. The buzzer would go again, and we'd get dessert. It's amazing how we took these things for granted. I

*Guy aged five, 1966.*

don't know what other families did, but that's what the Winships did! We probably weren't all that different from other middle-class white families in South Africa at the time.

Other than the maid, the nanny and the gardener, I didn't know any black people until I joined the army. My upbringing had been completely white. Lily-white. I went to a whites-only high school, Durban High; when I broke my collarbone playing rugby, I was treated at the hospital by white nurses and white doctors. There might have been a couple of black cleaners; I don't remember. My knowledge of black people and black culture was almost non-existent, apart from what we learned at school – and that, of course, was distorted through the lens of apartheid. There were six or seven grades in each year at high school; the top two or three grades studied Latin, and the bottom three or four grades learnt Zulu. It was a reflection of the wider South African society, I guess. I was in one of the top grades, so I learned Latin: *amo, amas, amat...*

Durban High School modelled itself on the English public school system, with its emphasis on discipline and sport. Sports were almost

*The Winship family, 1966. L to R: Allan ('Rusty'), Guy, Flora, Jonathan and Mark.*

more important than academic study: rugby in the winter and cricket in the summer. I was good at sport, but not a top player; good enough to participate, but not good enough to be a star. I was much the same in my academic work. I stayed out of trouble most of the time because I was competent academically, but I never got distinctions.

There was a strict uniform code, which included the length of our hair. We had to undergo 'prefect's inspections': we'd all line up, and the prefects or team captains would check that our hair was off our collars and our ears. There was a winter uniform and a summer uniform, but we always had to wear navy blue blazers and charcoal woollen trousers in the subtropical heat, and straw boaters – 'basher' hats, we used to call them.

Corporal punishment was still accepted in schools then. One of my primary school teachers stands out: Mrs Graham. She was a tall, thin woman with a beaky, wrinkled face and a terrifying gaze. She was my teacher in Standard 2, so that would've been my fourth year of formal schooling. I've always had terrible handwriting, and Mrs Graham was determined to improve my penmanship. She beat me black and blue. I was so upset that my mother went to the school and spoke to her. The teachers at Durban High School were also allowed to use the cane, and I got caned fairly regularly – for nothing in particular.

*Guy aged eleven in Standard 4 (equivalent of Year 6)
at Durban Preparatory High School, 1972.*

I remember my science teacher saying, 'Winship, what are you doing?'

'Sir, I'm doing nothing!'

'That's the trouble with you, Winship. You never do anything! Come here and I'll cane you!'

We used to joke about it, being beaten. We also joked about some of the teachers – but thinking about it now, the jokes weren't so funny. I guess we didn't think about it much at the time, but there were a couple of teachers at high school who were grooming kids for sex: being over-friendly, offering the boys gifts and favours, taking them on hikes up into the mountains 'to get to know them better' – that kind of thing. The joke was that you'd be called by a teacher – 'Come with me into the back room, boy. I'm going to punish you!' – to which the reply would be, 'Oh no, sir, I'd rather be caned!' We laughed about it then, but now, thinking back, I'm appalled.

When I was about fourteen or fifteen, I started exploring my spirituality, my religious beliefs. I wanted to engage more with the church, and one of the teachers, who claimed to be a Christian, invited me and another boy to go on an overnight hike with him. At the time, it seemed like a reasonable thing to do. But he got us to hike naked. He told us that it was natural, that we should free ourselves from our inhibitions. He said that he always hiked naked himself. Nothing actually happened; he didn't touch me or the other boy, and we went home the next day as if everything was fine. But I felt very uncomfortable. I never told my parents. I wondered if I was making more of it than I should. Perhaps it really had been just about being free and open and communing with nature. Perhaps there was nothing sexual in it. I guess I wasn't very sexually aware at fourteen; I was just beginning to discover my own sexuality at that age. There's no way I'd have had the confidence to complain. Can you imagine a fourteen-year-old in the 70s going to complain about a teacher? The teacher would've denied it. The other boy felt the same as me, very uncomfortable. We talked about it afterwards and agreed we'd have nothing more to do with that teacher. I would occasionally see him in the corridor and he would say hello, but I just avoided him. He was the teacher that the kids made jokes about. Until that incident, those jokes went over my head. I didn't take them seriously until then.

Thinking back, it's hard to know how much that incident affected me. I don't think it affected me sexually in any way, but that incident definitely coloured my view of the church. Together with stories that I heard later from friends about relationships between clergy and kids at school, that experience made me wary of organised religion. It also made me withdraw, pull back into my shell. I only came out of my shell again after finishing high school. That teacher was still at the school by the time I left.

I turned seventeen in my last year at school. I was one of the youngest in the class. I think I was pretty immature, both academically and physically, and I probably should have been in the year below. There was only one guy who was even younger than me in our year – a very good friend, Bronek Masojada. He was born in December, so he was three months younger than me. The two of us became good mates partly because we were by far the youngest in the class. We went on to university together. He did engineering, and then he won a Rhodes scholarship to Oxford. He's now the chief executive officer of Hiscox, a major insurance company in England. Last year, he made a donation of a million rand – about $100,000 – to our old high school. I'm not sure that I would've been so generous!

∞

My mother, Flora Herwood, was born in 1929 and grew up in a town called Springfontein, in what was then the Orange Free State. The family lived in an Afrikaans neighbourhood, so Afrikaans was literally my mother's tongue. Her father had emigrated to South Africa from either Germany or Lithuania – I'm not sure which – and he'd had to learn Afrikaans. He was Jewish, and my mother's mother may have been too, but that's not certain. What I do know is that the family denied their Jewishness and changed their surname from Herr to Herwood. There was a lot of anti-Semitism at that time: Prime Minister P.W. Botha had been a Nazi sympathiser during the Second World War, and there was a National Socialist government from 1948 until 1989, when F.W. de Klerk took over. The anti-Semitism was part of the widespread belief in the superiority of the Aryan race. That was South Africa then; that was national socialism. That was the environment my mother grew up in during and after the war years.

Her family had been very poor. Sometimes she and her brothers and sisters would go looking for food in rubbish bins. She left school at thirteen and never finished high school. Not long after she left school, the family moved from the Free State to Durban, where they learned to speak English. We always spoke English at home, but Mom wanted us all to speak Afrikaans at home one day a week: Thursdays, I remember, was Afrikaans day. My Afrikaans was never that great, though, because we grew up in an English-speaking area.

*Flora Winship on safari in East Africa, 1951.*

Mom didn't work outside the home; after my elder brother Mark was born, she didn't have a job. She was an artist, and she'd sell her paintings to raise money for charity. She was an active participant in our local community; she was once a guest speaker at my primary school. There was always that sense of community in our family. I learned from her that it's an important part of life.

Mom was very beautiful. Before she married my father in 1952, she won the Miss Durban beauty contest, and the prize was a safari in East Africa. I've got an old photograph of her on that safari, standing over the carcass of a zebra. It's pretty horrifying now, of course, but in those days shooting game was perfectly acceptable. For many years after she was married and had children, Mom would still occasionally get her photo in the paper. When she went to 'The July' – the big annual horse race, like the Melbourne Cup here in Australia – she'd sometimes get her picture taken as a former Miss Durban.

My father, Allan Rolleston ('Rusty') Winship, had a very different background. He grew up in Durban in a well-to-do colonial family. The Winships originally came from Whitley Bay near Newcastle, in northern England. His grandfather, Thomas Winship, came out to South Africa from England in the 1880s and was infamous for being a devout flat-earther. He even published a book on the subject, called *Zetetic Cosmogony*.

Like my mother, my father didn't finish high school. He became an electrician and started his own business, an electrical contracting and retail business selling stoves, fridges and other electrical appliances. When he was in his forties, he sold the business and made enough money to buy some property, and then he went back to study and got what was then called a 'government ticket' and joined the government as an inspector of public works. When he was about sixty-one, he had a mild stroke, so he retired and received a generous government pension. He and my mother used to talk about living on the SKIN method – spend kids' inheritance now! They went overseas seventeen years in a row after my dad retired. But in fact they were very tight with money, very careful. My father used to have these sayings, like 'Look after those pennies, and the pounds will take care of themselves', and 'I worry about money, so I don't have to worry about money.' He didn't like borrowing money, and he'd say, 'You should always get interest, never pay interest.'

My father was always a little distant, a little reserved. His mother's family, the Perkins, came from Lichfield, a cathedral city in Staffordshire in England. They were very reserved. I don't think my father could break away from that British reserve.

At the end of my matriculation year, my best mate Chris Hock and I hitchhiked to Cape Town. We had a great time – that fantastic sense of freedom you have as a young person, travelling away from home for the first time.

When I got back, we were sitting around the dining table as usual for dinner, and between 'pass the salt' and the general chit-chat, my mother said, quite casually, 'So, Guy, are you still a virgin?'

My father, choking on his glass of wine, gasped, 'My dear! Please!'

My father had a very dry sense of humour – probably part of his British heritage. A very good friend of his had a holiday home called Tandhalani, which in Zulu means 'Place of Love', and we used to go there on holiday. I remember once we were on our way to Tandhalani, and we were stranded in a torrential downpour. We couldn't keep driving – the road was completely awash, with mudslides and cars slipping all over the place. My mother was in tears, it was so bad, and my father told her, 'It's only rain, dear!'

I remember another thing he said, about a friend of his who got married four times: 'Everyone's got a hobby!'

My father remained quite reserved and undemonstrative until late in life. In the last few years, when I talked to him on the phone I'd always tell him I loved him, and he'd say that he loved me, too. We never expressed our affection for each other openly like that when I was growing up.

When I first got my diagnosis, I didn't tell my mother. That was in September 2013. My father had already died in 2011, when he was eighty-nine. After I'd had my left eye removed in 2013, I phoned Mom and told her, and I travelled to South Africa in February the following year to see her.

I pointed out my false eye to her, and she looked at me and said, 'Oh, that? There's nothing wrong with that! It looks perfect to me!' She was trying to be funny, trying to make light of it, but she'd been in tears on the phone when I first told her. She never mentioned it again.

Mom never knew that my cancer had metastasised. She died in June 2014, a few months before I received the news that the cancer had spread. She was spared that.

∞

It wasn't until 1998, when I was about thirty-seven, that I discovered that my mother had possibly been born Jewish. Jacqui and I were visiting my cousin Avril in a little village just outside Bristol in the west of England. Avril told me that she'd done some research into our grandparents because she wanted to apply for an ancestral visa to stay in the UK, and that's how she had discovered that our grandfather came from Europe and was Jewish.

When I went home, I confronted my mother about it.

Mom started to cry. 'Don't you still love me?' she said. 'I don't want to talk about it.'

'Of course I love you, Mom,' I said, 'but I'm interested.'

'I don't want to talk about it. I'm a Christian now.' There were a lot of tears, bitter tears. She refused to say any more.

There was an incident later when she denied that the Holocaust had ever taken place. After that, there were things that I felt I could never talk to her about. Every time I brought it up, from then until she died, she would never talk about her Jewish heritage.

I don't know if my father ever knew. Mom asked me never to talk to him about it. They're both dead now, so I can't ask him. I'm actually quite proud of my Jewish heritage, and when I lived in Uganda I began to explore my Jewishness further. Sometimes on Friday nights I'd go off to join Jewish friends at their homes for Shabbat. Candles would be lit at sunset and we would pray. My friends encouraged me to learn some of the Hebrew blessings, but I never succeeded in learning to recite them.

So: I was born partly Jewish, grew up Christian, and I choose to be agnostic. Since getting this diagnosis, Jacqui tells me that when I refer to myself as a Christian, I'm just hedging my bets! I proudly tell my kids that they're part Jewish, by blood at least. My son Thomas was interested in exploring it further, and at one stage he even thought about converting.

One of my earliest memories of starting to turn away from organised religion was when I witnessed the reaction of people to the appointment of Desmond Tutu as bishop of the Anglican church. I was about fifteen at the time and just starting to become a little more politically aware. Many of my parents' friends thought the idea of having a black bishop was completely ridiculous. 'A black bishop? Never!' The Anglicans from our neighbourhood – the white Anglicans – were appalled. They left the Anglican Church in droves and moved to the Congregationalist Church, which was the church my family attended. It opened my eyes to the prejudice around me in the name of Christianity and the reality of a deeply divided society.

∞

During the summer of 1976, when I was at the end of Standard 8 in high school – the equivalent of Year 10 in Australia – a few friends and I spent a couple of weeks camping beside a lake, about an hour and a half inland from Durban. The lake was Midmar Dam, a man-made lake with a campsite, and we stayed there over the Christmas holidays. That was the first time I'd stayed away from home for more than a few days at a time, away from my parents and my brothers, just with friends my own age. I'd been a boy scout and I'd been on camping trips before, but this was different: there were no adults. Our parents drove us there and then two weeks later came back to pick us up and take us home.

While we were there, I took a shine to this lovely, tall girl, Trudi Hock. I tried to chat her up, but when she discovered I was fifteen – three or four years younger than her – that was that. She put me firmly in my place! Then I met her younger sister, Barbara, and tried chatting her up too; but she was also older than me, so I didn't fare any better. So I got to know their younger brother, Chris Hock. We became firm friends on that camping holiday, and we're still best mates today.

Chris is a bit of an idealist, with boundless energy. Like me, I guess! He founded a rural housing facility as a non-profit organisation, and recently he worked on a microfinance project in the Congo. He and his wife, Claire, came to Australia to see me in 2016 because they weren't sure when they'd be able to see me again. It was a very special time with them.

∞

My folks had a granny flat at the back of their property. When I was in my teens, an Irish guy and his wife lived there. The Irishman introduced to me to surfing, and I became really keen. By the time I was at university, I spent most of my free time surfing.

My mother used to say, 'If it's a choice between surfing or university, you'll choose surfing every time!'

It was true. I'd run outside early in the morning and put my finger up to see which way the wind was blowing. If it was an offshore wind, or there wasn't a lot of wind, I'd go surfing. If the weather was bad, I'd go to university. That was one of the reasons it took me four years to get a three-year degree!

Surfing's not like other sports. It's very solitary: just you and the ocean. You don't need anyone else. It's pretty scary at first. As a surfer, you learn to manage that fear and see it as a challenge. You learn to read the waves, which ones to ride. You get hooked: riding a wave, then waiting and watching for the next one, riding that wave, then again watching for the next. Hour after hour. At eighteen, your fitness and your stamina are unbelievable.

In Zulu culture, there's a strong sense of connection between people and nature. A spiritual connection. I felt that connection with the ocean, sitting on my surfboard, surrounded by water, looking back at the land, paddling and planning. You get this wonderful sense of freedom. A feeling of peace. Surfing can be very soothing for one's soul.

Drugs were a big part of the surfing subculture. I was smoking a lot of marijuana myself at one stage. Some people got heavily into drugs, but not many. Most saw surfing as a healthy lifestyle thing. They'd be into vegetarianism, that kind of thing.

My old friend Stephen Matthews sent me a couple of photographs of the two of us from those days recently – blond hair, bleached by the sun, deeply tanned skin. We were on the beach near Durban. The photos must date from around 1981 or 1982. That was at the height of the apartheid years. The beaches were always busy, but there wasn't a black person in sight. Black people weren't allowed to go to those beaches. The only black people you saw around those beaches were street sweepers or cleaners. There were blacks-only beaches too, but they were in a completely different area, further away from central Durban and not as convenient.

*Guy catching a wave at Pasta Point, Maldives, 2009.*

Often the best waves are further away at the more remote beaches, and it's easier to catch more waves if you're away from the crowd. The further you are from people, the greater the connection with the sea… and of course the greater the chance of being attacked by sharks. But when you're young, you think you'll live forever.

Surfing was a big part of my life, but since moving away from Durban it's played a much smaller role. About eight years ago, Jacqui and the children and I went on a trip to the Maldives with Jacqui's family. We had a great time. I did some surfing, although I wouldn't say I surfed well – one needs to be fit to surf well! – but I did manage to catch a few waves. Since I lost my eye, I've been worried about the false eye falling out in the surf. It's a lot of work, making a false eye, and it cost about $2,500. There's also the risk of getting an infection if the eye came out in the sea. It may only be a small risk, but I don't want to take the chance.

I haven't surfed for more than two years now, but I found a couple of surfboards in my garage recently and I was thinking I might just take one out. It'd be good for my fitness, and if the surf's not too big, I might catch a wave or two.

∞

While I studied at university, I worked part-time at a bookmaker's in a small shopping centre in Isipingo, a satellite town south of Durban. There was a strong gambling culture there. A few mates and I worked there on Wednesdays and Saturdays from about eleven o'clock until about five. It was fairly well paid. My parents paid my university fees but they didn't pay for anything else, so this was my spending money. My folks had given me a car, a sky-blue VW beetle that had been my mother's for a while. When I needed money for petrol, I'd work at the bookmaker's.

There's nothing more materialistic than gambling. It's all about money. The bookmaker, whose name was Rob, was a foxy-faced fellow with a moustache and swept-back black hair flecked with grey. He laughed and joked around a lot, but it was a serious business. He would set the odds; the punters would come in and lay bets. I would often do the duplas – in other words, which horses would come first and second, in any order; and the trifectas – which pairs of two horses would come in the first three. We would follow what the TAB odds were. The TAB – the Totaliser Agency Board – was much like the TAB in Australia. The bets would all get pooled; ten per cent would go to the government as tax, ten per cent would go to the TAB as a fee, and eighty per cent would get shared amongst the winners. If the bets were spread across the board, the odds were in the favour of the bookmaker. Most of the time he's going to come out on top: he's not the one who's gambling, after all.

There was a strong sense of camaraderie between me and the friends who worked there. We'd get lifts together, and sometimes we'd take our surfboards and go and catch an early morning wave before heading off to work. On the way, we'd try and persuade as many pretty girls to come along as we could. But the gambling was ugly, really, to be honest. Isipingo had formerly been a 'white' town, but it was reallocated to Indians under the apartheid government's racial engineering policies. The part where we worked near the old railway track was overcrowded and poor. Most of the punters were working-class Indian men – artisans, tradesmen – just trying to make an extra dollar. I could smell the curry they'd eaten the night before and their sweat from the pressure of having put their savings on a long-shot horse. They'd drink a lot and get worked up as the afternoon wore on, and there'd be all kinds of bad behaviour – guys getting upset, hitting each other… Some of them would try to change their tickets to reflect a winner rather than a loser. It was terrible, really. The desperate look in their eyes. What they'd have to do when they went back home, what they'd have to say to their families. I imagined all kinds of things.

My mates and I tried to have as much fun as we could, but then one guy stole some money and got caught. The books didn't balance. Rob decided not to bring in the police, but he fired my mate. Things sort of fell apart after that. There's no loyalty in money. I wouldn't say it's the root of all evil, but it certainly didn't bring out the best behaviour in the punters, or in my mate, or in Rob. He'd be chain-smoking in his back office, with white dots on his cheekbones from the stress and the pressure. I heard he had a heart attack in his early forties, some years later, and I'm sure it was from the unrelenting pressure. Fifty thousand dollars could swing on a race – and there were eight races in a day. Just pure pressure. If you as the bookmaker won $50,000, you couldn't go and say to the punters, 'Hey, I've just made $50,000!' You've got to keep them on side because they are your customers. When they've just lost a whole lot of money you've got to commiserate with them, when you're secretly glad. And when they win, you can't swear and carry on; you've got to be nice to them to keep them coming back. It's an ugly business.

I don't gamble and I don't believe in gambling. Having said that, a year or two ago a friend told me a joke about this guy. Let's call him Fred. So Fred dies and goes to heaven, and he meets God. He says, 'You know, God, I've been good my whole life. I looked after my family. I looked after my community. I gave money to the church. I gave money to charity. I was good to my workers. I was good to my family. I never cheated on my wife. And now I'm here and I'm dead and you never let me win the lottery!'

And God said to Fred, 'Fred, you needed to meet me halfway. You should've bought a ticket!'

I really like that joke. In a way, it reflects my own thoughts about God. I'd like to believe in God. I like the idea of there being a good God, more than anything. I believe in good over evil, I guess. I hope there is a God: someone good who strengthens our resolve and makes us better people. But I also think, to be a better person, you've got to meet God halfway. So, two years ago, I started buying one ticket a week for the lottery. My theory is that your chances increase a lot by buying one ticket, but they don't increase very much by buying a second ticket – so, unlike Fred, I'm trying to meet God halfway. I haven't mentioned the lottery ticket in my prayers – yet! If there is an all-powerful God, He or She will know I've got a lottery ticket – so perhaps they'll meet me halfway too!

∞

University was liberating: going from the cloistered, beaten, regimented haircut life at high school to complete freedom. Wearing whatever I wanted, doing whatever I felt like. I grew my hair down to the middle of my back; I discovered girls and sex. I surfed most days. I smoked a lot of dope. I was popular – and probably a bit loud! I started to get involved in student politics. I joined various clubs and societies, played rugby a bit, surfed in a few of the university surfing competitions. And the girls! I have to confess that girls and surfing were the main focus of my life in my first two years at uni. Most mornings I'd head off to the beach early to catch a wave, maybe followed by a lecture or two. A lot of the time, I'd just hang out with friends around the students' refectory.

But of course, while I was having a great time, my studies suffered. By the end of my second year, I did so badly I got booted out of uni. So, at nineteen, I was forced to join the South African army for two years. Conscription was compulsory for white males in South Africa at that time. You were required to serve a total of four years: the first two years continuously and the second two years in three-month stints.

There was a famous anti-war song which was very popular at that time about going to Vietnam. It's called 'Nineteen'. There's a bit at the beginning of the song which says the average age of a soldier in the Second World War was twenty-six; the average age of a soldier in Vietnam was nineteen. It was quite poignant for me at that time, that song, being nineteen myself when I was conscripted.

In hindsight, if I was going to do military service, I should've done it straight from high school. And if I wasn't going to do it, I should've just left the country. My mother actually said to me, 'Why don't you go and stay with your aunt in Canada?' But I was too young and innocent and I just didn't think about those things. I wasn't really politically aware at that age. I thought, it can't be that bad, can it?

# 2

# A developing consciousness

'What atonement is there for blood spilt upon the earth?' – Aeschylus

After about five months of military training, I was thrown as a nineteen-year-old conscript into the middle of the South African border war in Angola. I landed in a helicopter with two other platoons, two hundred kilometres inside Angola. It was hot and dry, with searing blue skies. I remember the terror, the sense of disorientation. Wondering whether I would get out alive.

At its heart, the war was about independence for what was then South West Africa, and is now Namibia. The South West African People's organisation (SWAPO) and its guerrilla arm, the People's Liberation Army of Namibia (PLAN), were fighting for independence and South Africa was fighting against it. As South Africa struck further and further into Angola, chasing PLAN and seeking out its bases, the war merged into the Civil War in Angola, which in turn was a proxy conflict of the Cold War. By the time I was conscripted in the early 1980s, South African forces had penetrated deep into Angola.

Even after all this time, I don't like to talk about my time fighting that grubby little war. It was just terrible. If a farmer was found to have a gun, he was shot. He and his family would be killed. SWAPO hid explosives in farmyards, or along paths. They would set tripwires across roads. One of the guys in our platoon opened a gate and lost his left hand. I can't even begin to describe how bad it was. There was a corporal in our platoon… Oh God, it was just horrible. I've never told anyone about this before, but the corporal collected ears. Human ears. He compared the number of ears he'd collected with the corporal from another platoon.

*At the Namibia (then South West Africa) –Angola border just prior to entering Angola, July 1981. Guy recalls taking this photograph (illegally) because of the sign: 'Don't die for your country, let the enemy die for it'.*

They were having a competition. I can't remember exactly how long we were in Angola, but I have a clear memory of leaving. We had to cross a wide-open area, at the Namibia–Angola border. It was called the Cut. It had been blasted with Agent Orange and there was no vegetation for about eight hundred metres. You could see for miles, left and right, as you walked across. We'd just reached the military airport and we were all lined up for the flight back. Then I saw it: a string of human ears in the corporal's khaki duffel bag. He closed the bag quickly and I only saw it for a moment, but I'll never forget it. I heard later that one of the corporals got arrested and prosecuted, but perhaps that was just a rumour. There was never any official announcement.

That's the terrible thing about war: you're trained to kill and to be as barbaric as you can. You have to shoot and kill people before they kill you. It's kill or be killed. But there are still rules. Even in war, there are codes of conduct. Collecting ears…somehow that transgresses any sense of decent behaviour, even in war. It's unbelievable how inhuman one can become.

And then you come back to so-called civilisation. You feel weird. Displaced. Arriving home, there was a sense of alienation. First, we were back at the base, then a week later we were given leave and arrived home. From seeing those ears on a string to being taken out by my parents to dinner at the Royal, a fancy restaurant in a five-star hotel in Durban, with its waiters and white tablecloths and silver cutlery. From seeing a mate's hand blown off to having to think about which spoon to use.

There's a lot of talk of the friendships you make in war, and I did form friendships with some of the guys in my platoon. But those friendships weren't deep. I felt that we had nothing in common except the fact that we were all conscripts and we'd been thrown together in this war. What we did have in common was hating the army. In the first year, it wasn't a case of hating the army, it was a case of survival. I resisted making lasting friendships because I didn't want to be reminded of this time in the future. We all deal with things in different ways, and my way of dealing with being in the army was denial. I just wanted it to end. I wanted to get out.

I've never wanted to talk about my time in the army. Even thirty-five years later, I still have strong memories of the hurt, the fear, the alienation, the exasperation, sometimes anger – and of course guilt and shame. Happiness, too, I have to admit: happiness at surviving. Survival is always a good thing.

I'm ashamed of having been a part of that war. When I got my diagnosis, that story about how I fired a smoke bomb by mistake instead of a mortar round was the one story I told Jacqui and Thomas about my war days – in fact, it's the only story I've ever told them. It feels like a gift, to be granted all this time since then. I could so easily have died.

∞

After those two years of military service, I went back to university for two years and finished my degree. I was much more focused this time around. I finished my undergraduate degree with honours, and then I

*Flora, Guy and Allan ('Rusty') at Guy's undergraduate graduation, Durban, 1984.*

applied to do a master's in town planning. I made a deliberate choice to study something practical and vocational, and I was drawn to the idea of creating something tangible.

My university years were a time of growing political awareness, particularly around social justice issues. I started doing some voluntary teaching in townships on the outskirts of Durban, teaching English literature to classes of two or three hundred kids – anything from George Orwell to George Eliot. I'd done a year of English literature at university, and I wondered if that was enough to qualify me. But the people running the voluntary program said, 'It doesn't matter. We take whoever we can get. Off you go!' So, with my basic lesson plan in one hand and the steering wheel of my battered old VW beetle in the other, I'd take myself off to the townships to teach at a couple of schools.

There were two main townships near Durban at that time: Umlazi in the south, and Kwamashu in the north. It was a good hour's drive there, mostly along dirt roads, and another hour back.

It wasn't easy, trying to keep control of a class of two or three hundred kids. The kids were naughty, just like any normal teenagers: some kids at the back of the class would tease me or try to pick up the girls. Their English was really weak – but my Zulu was even worse! For those kids, English was a second language and their understanding was pretty rudimentary. I started off trying to tell them about alliteration and pathos, but then I realised that for them to understand Dickens, or George Eliot, or *1984*, I just had to focus on telling the story. I'd bring props that I'd prepared during the week and show them pictures of the characters – you know, the man and the woman, if it was *Middlemarch*, say – and just tell them the basic plot, so that they'd at least know that. I'd say to them, 'When you come to write your exam, just tell the story!'

Those kids were supposed to have their own teachers during the week, but that often didn't happen. The teachers just didn't show up. That's still true in many places. Even today, there are an estimated one million kids in South Africa – mostly black kids in rural areas – who don't get an education because no one turns up to teach them. It's a complete tragedy. Cry the beloved country, is all I can say.

Teaching those township kids wasn't easy, but not only because of the poor infrastructure and the huge classes. It was also knowing that the army or police were just down the road. There was a state of emergency on at that time and tension was simmering below the surface. Sometimes there'd be violent outbreaks, particularly in the townships. People were fed up with living under apartheid and they were starting to rebel. You couldn't blame them; their living conditions were terrible. They had no infrastructure, no facilities, no services, no decent education, no jobs. They were being treated like second-class citizens. That's what they were, in the eyes of the state: second-class citizens. And they'd had enough. The response of the apartheid state was to clamp down hard. They were very militaristic, figuratively and literally.

I used to start my class at nine o'clock in the morning, so things were usually fairly quiet at that time. Sometimes there'd be police patrolling the streets, in their blue and grey uniforms, driving around in their bakkies – what Australians call utes. The bakkies were partly covered with steel mesh. Any scuffles or signs of trouble, and the police would throw people into the back. I remember walking to school one

Saturday morning, past a small group of police: two whites and one black. The black policeman was standing apart from the whites because of segregation. Their bakkie was open at the back and I saw that it was splattered with blood. I just kept walking, looking straight ahead, to go and talk to two or three hundred kids about George Orwell.

Sometimes there would also be army units in the township. Most of the soldiers were young conscripts, kids of eighteen or nineteen in their brown uniforms, standing on the side of the road, slouching around with their automatic rifles – Israeli-designed automatic rifles, with a curved magazine containing thirty rounds of 5.56 ammunition. I got to know these weapons very well during my own conscription. I could take one apart, clean it and reassemble it – in the dark. I laugh when I see people in the movies hiding behind a wall to shelter from automatic gunfire. Automatic rifles can shoot straight through a house, straight through five people. And putting this incredibly powerful weapon in the hands of eighteen-year-old conscripts! And the black kids – understandably angry and frustrated – would sometimes throw stones at the soldiers, with no thought of how much of a risk they were taking. The consequences for those young white conscripts of shooting someone – most likely killing them – would be just terrible. I can't blame them for finding themselves in that situation; they didn't want to be there, and they had to protect themselves, I guess. And I couldn't blame the young black kids, either, for wanting to throw stones. I couldn't blame them for their anger and frustration. They had no hope. They couldn't get a decent education; they weren't allowed to go to university, no matter how bright they were. They were severely restricted in what jobs they could get. Seeing that was part of the reason why I became politicised. It was just a tragedy.

∞

When I was in the final year of my master's, I made up my mind that I wasn't going to do the second two years of military service. I'd become more socially and politically aware by then and much more conscious of social justice issues. I'd been able to defer my second two years of military service while I was studying, but as soon as I completed my master's degree in 1988, that deferment was no longer valid.

I've never been a particularly introspective person; reflection isn't something I've done naturally. But there have been points in my life that I reflect on – points that have led me to where I am now – when I've made choices, and those choices have led to seminal changes. One such point was when I made the decision not to serve the second two years of military service. I didn't have to face the consequences of that decision until the following year, when I started working for a development bank, the KwaZulu Finance and Investment Corporation (now known as the Ithala Bank). The penalty at that time for refusing to do military service was two-for-one: two years' imprisonment for every year that you missed. If I'd been found guilty of breaking the law, I'd have had to face four years' imprisonment. Four years in an African jail can literally be a death sentence. It was a terrifying prospect.

∞

I became actively engaged with the African National Congress through my friendship with a colleague at the development bank, Tami Ngwenya. Before that, while I was still studying for my master's, I'd considered myself a supporter of the ANC, but I only became a member after Tami offered to introduce me. The ANC was still banned as a political organisation at that time and was working underground, and you could get arrested and sent to jail simply for being a member. Tami understood from my political views that I was a supporter, and one day he asked me if I was interested in becoming a member. I told him that I was definitely interested, so he helped to get me signed up and I joined an underground branch in Durban, down in the city. I still have my ANC membership card today.

My involvement with the ANC strengthened my resolve not to serve the second stint of military service. It wasn't until 1989 that the issue came to a head. One of the benefits of working for the development bank was they had a low-interest loan scheme for their staff, so I bought a three-bedroom apartment in Durban, in a suburb called Morningside. A couple of close friends – Wayne Tammadge and Sioux McKenna, who remain very close friends to this day – moved in to help pay the rent. In those days, Sioux was pretty wild and very radical; she is now a professor at Rhodes University in Grahamstown, South Africa.

In August '89 Sioux discovered she was pregnant. She'd had a pregnancy test and brought home the report confirming the result. Sioux and Wayne had only been together a few months, so the news was a bit of a shock. At around the same time, I received a call-up notice from the military. With Sioux's permission, I borrowed her pregnancy test report and rushed off to the local headquarters of the South African Army.

I ran into a lieutenant, waved the pregnancy test report at him, and said, 'Look, I've got terrible news! My girlfriend is pregnant! I can't come. This is terrible!'

And this lieutenant – I think he was the adjutant of the unit I was supposed to be with, Durban Light Infantry – sat me down in his office and gave me a two-hour lecture on why we should go ahead and have the baby, and how I should stand by my girlfriend, even if things between us weren't good.

I don't know what he thought of me; I must've looked pretty scruffy at the time, in jeans and a T-shirt. I don't know if he was religious, but he was certainly anti-abortion, and he was obviously concerned about my predicament.

So, on the basis of that pregnancy test, I was granted a deferment for that year. I felt a little false; I generally believe in being honest, but this was a desperate situation! When I gave Sioux back the pregnancy test, I told her that if she got a phone call from the army, she was to please tell them that we were living together. We were living in the same apartment, so she didn't have to lie.

That deferment bought me a bit more time to work out what I was going to do, but I only had till the end of that year. By then, I was absolutely determined not to undertake any further military service. I started looking around for support and I came across Howard Varney, a young articled clerk in his final year of law studies. Howard was doing some work as a volunteer with the End Conscription Campaign, giving legal advice to young white men who qualified for conscription.

Howard sat me down in a shabby room with beige walls and chipped paint in the campaign office at the Ecumenical Centre, an old Victorian building in downtown Durban. The police and security forces were constantly bugging them, literally, as well as arresting them and harassing them in various ways.

Howard said, 'Look, you make the decision. Are you going to go, or aren't you going to go?'

I said, 'I'm not going to do it.' It felt like a huge decision for me back then.

'Well, okay, so you've made the decision. You're committed to that. You know there might be consequences?'

'It doesn't matter what the consequences are, I'm not going to do any more military service.'

Howard nodded. 'Well, there are two ways to do this. The hard way or the soft way. The hard way is you go and take a stand. You tell the newspapers, you try to get onto radio and TV. You write letters, you speak out publicly. Whatever your reasons, you say you're going to stand up to the apartheid government.'

I had a very good friend, Grant Myrdal, whose older brother Brett had refused to do military service. Brett had done it the hard way: he'd spoken at universities and in other public places. He'd been arrested and harassed mercilessly. I saw what a toll it had taken on him and his family.

Howard saw me hesitate. Then he said, 'Or you do it the soft way. The soft way is where you duck and dive, you avoid, you obfuscate, you try to stay one step ahead of the law and get off on technicalities.'

I said to Howard, 'I think I'm going to go the soft way.'

∞

The authorities caught up with me around the middle of 1990. Nelson Mandela had been released in February and things were starting to open up. At the same time, the violence had escalated and South Africa was on the brink of civil war. The police were on the streets, especially in the townships. One of the things I'd have had to do, if I'd gone back to do military service, would be to police the townships. I wasn't prepared to do that.

That decision not to do my second two years of military service was one of the toughest decisions of my life, despite my convictions. Some members of my family wouldn't talk to me – especially when they heard I was actively involved in the ANC. That was quite confronting.

Conscription notices were delivered by registered mail, so the authorities needed your current address to serve the notice. I hadn't notified them of my change of address, so one day in June 1990 the military police turned up at my parents' house and demanded to know where I could be found. My father gave them the address where I was working. He believed I should do my military service simply because that's what the government wanted. What I believed didn't matter. I loved my parents very much and they brought me up to think critically, but they weren't intellectuals. My father supported the white separatist government. He believed you shouldn't question the state. We had a fight about it.

I told him, 'This has nothing to do with whether you think I'm right or wrong. This is about supporting me as your son – whether you agree with me or not!' I'm ashamed to say I shouted at him. I guess I thought that if he'd been more loyal he could've simply said he didn't know where I was. It would've been easy enough.

The following day, the military police arrived at my office and served me with a subpoena to appear in court – not a military court, but a civil court. This was a shock: I'd expected my case would go before a military court. Getting prosecuted in a civil court would mean getting a criminal record, which would have had serious long-term consequences. It would mean, for example, that I could never be a director of a company in South Africa. I had no intention of leaving South Africa at that stage, so it felt like they were throwing the book at me.

On Howard Varney's advice, I pleaded not guilty to all charges of refusing to do military service, treason, fighting the apartheid state, and all the other vicious charges that they accused me of – but I pleaded guilty to the fact that I hadn't given the army my change of address, so the subpoena hadn't been properly served. And I won! I had the choice of a fine of 100 rand – the equivalent of $100 or so in today's money – or ten days in jail. I spoke with the prosecutor afterwards and he told me my case was treated as a 'misdemeanour'. I didn't realise this at the time, but that meant that it didn't constitute a criminal record.

I managed to go on avoiding conscription for another year or two. I moved again, a couple of times, and again I didn't let the authorities know my change of address.

I also said to my father, 'If anyone calls again, please don't tell them where I live. Say you don't know!'

He must've taken to heart what I'd said to him previously because that's just what he did. The next time the military police called, he told them he'd lost contact with me.

I thought, if I'm charged again with failing to give them my change of address, what would I get? Twice the number of days in jail, or double the fine? I kept ahead of them, or maybe they just gave up on me; I don't know. I never got another piece of paper.

∞

After the release of Nelson Mandela in February 1990, the ANC was unbanned and I started being much more open about my political affiliation. In 1993, in the lead-up to the election, I worked as a volunteer for the ANC, attending meetings, working on electioneering administration, and helping people to register on the electoral roll so they could vote. I also spent a lot of my free time putting up posters, including in white neighbourhoods. The response of some white people was unbelievable. I was spat at, abused, called names. Some of my relatives felt that by joining the liberation movement I had betrayed my folk, my family and community. One of my uncles cut me off and refused to have anything to do with me for a year or two. He was vociferous in his condemnation of me.

My parents were much more accepting. They shrugged and said, 'Your politics aren't the same as ours, but that's okay.'

Mom would roll her eyes, but she loved me enough to forgive me anything.

Until the first democratic election was held, no one knew how much support there would be for the liberation movement. As well as the ANC, other groups were also striving to gain political support: groups like the Pan African Congress, the South African Communist Party, and the Congress of South African Trade Unions. Opinion polls were conducted, of course, but the level of support for all those organisations was untested because the majority South Africans hadn't previously had the vote. As far as the white community was concerned, support for the ANC was negligible. Some estimates put it at about half of one per cent of the total white population. It was the start of my sense of alienation, both from the white community, many of whom still clung to apartheid, and from the black community. I couldn't relate to much of Zulu culture; I found it highly patriarchal and at times misogynist, to be honest. That sense of alienation, together with the escalating violence, contributed to my decision about five years later to leave South Africa permanently. My wife Jacqui used the analogy of the frog in boiling water: because you're living with violence every day, it becomes normal. You don't notice that it's escalating, that the water is getting hotter. The violence was a big part of why we decided to leave South Africa.

∞

My decision not to complete my military service was life-changing. I still consider it the most significant step I've taken in terms of acting on my beliefs. It was about deciding what's not acceptable to you as a person. It was about where to draw the line in the sand. From then until now, that decision set me on a path that has determined the work I do and the choices I've made in so many ways.

That decision was the result of many things: my upbringing, my growing awareness of the inequality and injustices of life in apartheid South Africa, and the progressive thinking of the academic staff and students at university where I did my master's degree. But it was the two years I'd spent in the military, eight or nine years before that, fighting in Angola – that's what really changed my thinking.

I grew to believe that freedom in South Africa meant freedom of choice and freedom to vote. I believe in democracy and that the majority should have the vote and decide their own future. But I also believe in the rule of law and I believe in meritocracy. I have deeply mixed feelings about what's happened to South Africa. One million kids are still not receiving an education. That's South Africa today. There's as much inequality now as there has ever been; it's just less clearly along racial lines. Now, it's more closely linked to economic privilege.

All that work I did, teaching in the township, putting up posters for the ANC before the first democratic elections and getting spat on or having things thrown at me by white South Africans in my neighbourhood, or facing up to that magistrate in the court in downtown Durban…trying to do work that would make the world a better place… Maybe it's been about trying to make things right: atonement for taking those lives in Angola all those years ago. Who knows? I don't know how you become who you are. The pieces just come together in the end.

# 3

# Love and loss

'Happiness is a decision' – David Savage

When I was twenty-five and about halfway through my master's degree, I got married to my first wife. It was a volatile relationship – a constant cycle of break-ups and make-ups. Living with her, I came to realise that I don't like volatility in my personal relationships. I didn't like the constant cycle of arguments, remorse, kissing and making up. It was completely exhausting. You don't think of these things when you're twenty-five, but reflecting back on it, I'm sure that was a large part of what was wrong for me with that relationship.

My first wife and I were just so different. Her background was very unstable: her parents were divorced following a very unhappy marriage. Her dad had made money in business, then lost it, then made it again…a bit of a cycle of boom and bust. I'm exaggerating a little, but there was a lot of instability in her family. She had big issues with trust. I thought that marriage would give her security.

A couple of years after we were married, she had an affair. I guess it was her way of forcing us to confront the fact that the relationship wasn't working. She told me about the affair; she didn't know how else to bring about a separation. I don't know whether the affair in itself was the cause of the break-up; I think some relationships just aren't meant to be. We tried to reconcile, and we kept sleeping together for a while, but it became increasingly obvious that the marriage was over. We got divorced a year later, in April 1989.

In those days, you had to go to the Supreme Court in Durban to be granted a divorce, which was an experience in itself. I remember the courtroom: all wood panelling, very traditional, very conservative. It felt quite surreal. A murder case had been heard in the same court the day before, and I felt the ghosts of those other experiences in that room. The whole thing took fifteen minutes. I went to take the stand and my lawyer asked me a few questions. I'd been coached in what to say. The only question the judge asked me was, 'Is there any possibility of reconciliation?', and I had to say 'No' very firmly, because if I opened the door to the possibility of reconciliation, they wouldn't have granted us a divorce.

That was around the time – at the end of '89 – when the government announced that Nelson Mandela was going to be released. And then on 2 February 1990, when he was released: all those famous pictures and TV shots of him walking out of the gates of the prison, hand in hand with Winnie Mandela. It felt like the world had shifted.

In my personal life, I felt pretty battered and bruised. I struggled with trying to reconcile my sense of hurt, of failure; the knowledge that this relationship hadn't succeeded.

∞

But good things can come from pain. After my experience with my first marriage, I was hesitant to go into another relationship without a lot more thought. I wanted it to be a deliberate decision. A balanced choice. I'd learned some big lessons, like the importance of good communication, the need to deal with differences and conflicts early. Accepting that if things aren't working out, they're just not working out – it's no use apportioning blame. These are important lessons. Even after twenty-seven years, from the end of that first marriage till now, those lessons remain. There's nothing like a burning knot in your heart to drive home what makes a good relationship.

I first met Jacqui Savage when I was still married to my first wife. We met at the house of a mutual friend, Mark Notcutt. It was his birthday and he'd arranged a breakfast with a group of mates.

Jacqui was pretty unimpressed with me at that first meeting. We

*Guy and Jacqui, Durban, 1991.*

got into a fight over teachers' salaries, which she felt more qualified to comment on than me. We met up again about a year later, when I was getting over my divorce. Jacqui says she was much more impressed with me this time and joked to a friend that I'd make 'good husband material', but not for her – at least, not yet! She set me up on a blind date with a friend of hers, but there was no spark between her friend and me, so nothing came of it. With Jacqui, on the other hand, I certainly felt a spark, but she was living with her boyfriend at the time in a granny flat at the back of Mark's parents' house.

When Jacqui broke up with her boyfriend a few months later, she came around in tears to see my housemate Sioux, who was Jacqui's best friend and still is to this day. She asked Sioux if she could stay for a few days while she sorted herself out. Sioux talked to me about it. No problem, I said. So Jacqui moved into the spare room.

After a couple of days, I invited her out to dinner to cheer her up. I told her if she wore something sexy, I'd take her somewhere expensive. Well, she did wear something sexy, and I did take her to an expensive restaurant – expensive for me at the time! We'd both clearly bounced back better than we thought. A lot of our friends told us that we were on the rebound. We still laugh about that. It's certainly been a long rebound – twenty-six years!

'It didn't take long for romance to bloom,' Jacqui says. 'It's a sign of what a gentleman Guy is that the first time I made a pass at him he turned me down as I was drunk and he thought I might regret it when I sobered up! This only made me more interested, and we were soon in a relationship which all our friends thought was doomed to fail given that we were both on the rebound from long-term relationships. I guess we proved them wrong! We were engaged within a year and married six months after that. And yes, Guy has indeed proved to be good husband material!'

One of the lessons I learned from my first marriage was that while physical attraction is important – and certainly I was attracted to Jacqui! – on its own it's not enough. This time round, I was more conscious of other things: the importance of shared values, for example. From the start, I had the sense that our values were similar – our attitudes to money, for example, and to social justice, and our approach to relationships in general. We also had similar backgrounds: Jacqui had a secure, happy upbringing. Her family background was a lot like mine: secure and stable. Jacqui's parents were still together; there had never been any serious domestic issues. In terms of money, both Jacqui's and my parents were financially stable. We were both solidly middle class; maybe better off than average. I was very conscious of the differences between Jacqui's family and my first wife's family; I was much more aware of the important non-physical issues.

Jacqui and I were married on 4 April 1992 in a beautiful old Methodist church. Neither of us is religious, but Jacqui liked the idea of getting married in church. As I was divorced, we had to look around for a church that would marry us. The Methodists didn't really care about whether couples had been married previously, so we got married there. The reception was held at Jacqui's parents' house on the north side of Durban, overlooking the sea. They erected a marquee in the garden next to the swimming pool. I gave a speech and told a little story about my father telling me that the secret to a successful marriage is to take control early on. Everyone laughed, and then I followed that

*Guy and Jacqui on their wedding day, Jamison Park, Durban, 4 April 1992.*

up by saying, 'Of course, Jacqui is a faster learner than I am!' – which made everyone laugh even more! Jacqui was very eloquent in her speech, with references to various literary works, and she danced with her ninety-three-year-old grandfather. It was something he'd always wanted to do: dance with his beautiful granddaughter at her wedding. It was really wonderful.

Our honeymoon was in Kenya, which had only recently reopened its doors to South Africans following the lifting of apartheid sanctions. We stayed at the Hilton in Nairobi for one night and then spent a week at the beautiful Serena Beach Hotel, north of Mombasa. From there, we went back to Nairobi and stayed at the New Stanley Hotel. The Stanley has a fascinating history. It was named after the explorer, Sir Henry Morton Stanley – the one who found Livingstone. Ernest Hemingway stayed there a few times and worked on *The Green Hills of Africa* and *The Snows of Kilimanjaro*. Various dignitaries, royals and film stars have also stayed there. The hotel is also well-known for this noticeboard, like a poste-restante, where people leave messages and letters. Some of the notes and mail have been there for years, waiting for someone to come by and pick them up. People leave all kinds of messages there: messages like 'Jane, we met in Tanzania and I think I love you! Contact me', or 'Bob, you bloody crook, you still owe me £10!' Quite fascinating.

It's been a good marriage. Very stable, very secure. Very loving. We're highly compatible. Soulmates, some would say. Some people might even say boring! But the stability is good.

Jacqui describes her relationship with Guy as 'great friends who make each other laugh'. She recalls an incident in the early years of their marriage when they were still living in Durban. 'Guy came home from work one lunchtime, and I was up a ladder painting the walls of the lounge room. Having been to an official meeting that morning, he was wearing a formal suit and tie. As I leaned down from the ladder to kiss him, I dislodged the tin of bright yellow paint from the top step of the ladder – and tipped it over his head! He was quite a picture! Instead of getting upset, we both laughed hysterically!

'I've also been subjected to years of his bad jokes – with him often laughing so much that I can't even hear the punchline. He used to read to me sometimes, and one night we were lying in bed and he was reading me *Adrian Mole*. He got to the bit about longing for Wolverhampton and started laughing so hysterically he couldn't go on reading. I still only have to mention Wolverhampton for us both to burst out laughing again!

'I have so many memories of all our laughs together...and of all the cups of coffee he has made me over the years! – definitely his language of love.'

Being able to trust your partner is really important. Now that I've got this cancer, that's even more important. What you get out of a relationship reflects what you put into it, I guess. It's a huge challenge for Jacqui, living with someone who has many days of pain. Never mind the pain, but a whole lot of side effects – the nausea and the skin rash and the thyroid going...the list goes on and on. She's been incredible during this whole process. I would've done the same for her, of course.

But going back to when we first met and thinking about the things that were important beyond the attraction: I hadn't thought about things like supporting your partner through the really hard times. I took those things for granted, probably because my own parents had been happily married. Jacqui's strength and support from the time that I was diagnosed with this cancer has been amazing. She has been my 'medical supervisor', researching all possible treatment options and finding the best professionals and procedures to keep me alive over the last three years. It's been really tough for her, especially as she's lost both her brother Tim and her father since my diagnosis. Cancer is an ugly, messy, bloody business – but Jacqui's love and care have helped to make it bearable.

∞

When I first met Jacqui, she was heavily involved in sailing. Her family were all keen sailors and her brother Bruce represented South Africa in two Olympics. Jacqui wasn't in the same league, but she did compete in a couple of world laser sailing championships – in Morocco in 1997 and in Holland the following year.

It was after the regatta in Holland that we decided we'd have kids. I'd always wanted kids; Jacqui was less keen, but I talked her into it. I'd always imagined myself as having children, but Jacqui hadn't. Kids change things. I guess she wasn't sure if the change would be for the better or for the worse. Of course, the kids are central to our lives now; probably half our conversations are about them. If we ever go out for dinner, a romantic dinner with just the two of us, all we talk about for two hours are the kids. That's what you do.

We were married for eight years before we had children. Although Jacqui had been reluctant to have kids, she fell in love with them the moment they were born. They were both born naturally, but both were six or seven weeks premature. With Thomas, we decided that we'd have a natural birth at home: a water birth, with music and incense and a doula. We were staying at my parents' house; they were away, travelling overseas. We'd sold our own house in anticipation of working internationally – either somewhere else in Africa, or possibly in Cambodia.

One morning Jacqui woke up and said, 'Oh! The bed's wet!'

'Not a problem,' I said. 'It's probably just the pressure on your bladder. But you'd better go and see the doctor. I'm off to work.' It didn't occur to me that Jacqui could be in labour. She wasn't due for another seven weeks. So off I went to work.

An hour or so later, I got a phone call from the obstetrician. 'Mr Winship, I'm ringing to tell you your wife is here at the hospital and her waters have broken.'

Jacqui had driven herself to the hospital. I thought, no! This can't be happening. It's too early! The baby's not due yet! I rushed straight to the hospital and I was there with Jacqui when Thomas was born.

I think back to a story my father told. He and my mother were on honeymoon and they were out horse riding, and Mom got thrown off her horse. They got her to the hospital and the doctor said to the nurse, 'Quick, get a glass of brandy!' The nurse rushed off and got a glass of brandy and brought it back, and Mom said, 'I'm not drinking that!' and the doctor said, 'It's not for you, it's for your husband!' That's what I felt like. We were going to have this natural birth, a water birth, at home, and we ended up at the hospital.

Jacqui was in a lot of pain. She asked for an epidural, which of course meant she needed an anaesthetist – but they couldn't get hold of one right away. Jacqui kept asking when the anaesthetist was going to get there. Then she'd have another contraction, and she'd ask again, and eventually she ended up yelling, 'Where's the fucking anaesthetist?'

She got the epidural in the end, thank heavens, and Thomas was born by vacuum extraction. I must admit I felt a bit pale and wobbly when Jacqui was getting her stitches. Watching it being done, I thought, oh my God! I need that glass of brandy!

∞

I've recently read *Being Mortal*: it's about ageing and dying and mortality, what's important in life and what's not. In terms of my own life, the things that have been important, the really big things that trigger strong emotions: I guess they were getting married, divorced, and remarried. Starting a charity from scratch. Being told I was likely to die within a year.

The other big-ticket items in my life didn't happen overnight. Like falling in love with my children: that took time. I didn't fall in love with them the moment they were born. It happened gradually. I helped take care of them, of course, but I didn't really engage with them until they were a bit older. Now, my kids are incredibly precious to me, and sometimes I treat them as though they're balls of glass that could be broken at a touch. At other times, I think I'm too hard on them: I can be impatient, vehement. I overreact to small things. It's been really tough for them, having a father with terminal cancer. It's made me acutely aware of how much I love them. They're both beautiful human beings. The idea that I won't see them grow into adults is very painful.

Thomas is eighteen now. He and I are similar in many ways. We're both passionate about social justice, politics – especially American politics – and cars! We share the same quirky sense of humour. Both of us tune into other people's feelings easily, although – like lots of blokes – we don't discuss emotions very much. I know that next year he'll go off on his own to stay in college at university, but for now it's great having him around. He has done a lot of research on my cancer and possible treatments and side effects. I think it might've encouraged his interest in a medical career. If that's where he ends up, I know he'll make a great doctor.

Brontë is fifteen and quite different from her brother, although equally wonderful. She's feisty, emotionally robust, highly organised, intelligent. She's also very straightforward: she calls a spade a spade. I really admire that. She also seems to me quite self-sufficient and independent; perhaps she needs the approval of other people less than Thomas and me. She knows that I have terminal cancer, of course, but

*Jacqui's fiftieth birthday celebration with Winship and Savage family members on a South Pacific cruise, April 2016. L to R: Joliette, Jacqui's mother; Pauline, wife of Jacqui's late brother Tim; Lyn, wife of Bruce; Sue, wife of Mark; Bruce, Jacqui's brother; Mark, Guy's elder brother; Guy; David, Jacqui's father; and Jacqui.*

we've never discussed it in any depth. She was just eleven years old when my cancer metastasised; that's really young to be told that your father is going to die. Thankfully, I've been around for longer than the medics predicted. I'd love to see her go to her school formal in three years' time: that will be a significant milestone. I know it'll be a very special occasion for her, and she'll look even more beautiful than usual that night. But in any event, she knows how much I love her. I've often heard her tell people, 'My father will do anything for me!' – and she's right!

Having a terminal illness makes you think about what you want to do with whatever time you have left. A big thing for me was that I wanted to travel with my children: to share experiences with them, make memories. We've managed to fit in a lot of travel since my diagnosis in November 2014. We travelled to Europe and the UK, and to the United States; we went on a cruise to the South Pacific with family and friends for Jacqui's fiftieth birthday; we did a tour of Uluru and slept in swags, along with our good friends the Suntups

*Guy's son, Thomas, with Mark, New Caledonia, April 2016.*

and Hawkeswoods; and we've done a couple of trips back to South Africa to spend time with special friends there. We've cycled around Paris, Barcelona, Versailles and Boston, and climbed St Peter's Basilica in Rome (where we lost Thomas – but that's another story!). Brontë and I have been to the top of Table Mountain in Cape Town. We went to see *Wicked* on Broadway in New York; Thomas and I have taken the ferry to Alcatraz and toured the Colosseum in Rome. So many amazing experiences that I'm sure they'll remember forever. I think all the travel we've done together has matured them, given them a bigger perspective on life.

∞

It's amazing how everything is relative. Before I lost my eye, I would've thought losing an eye would be terrible. When I did lose my eye, I didn't think it was so terrible. Then, a year later, when the cancer metastasised, losing an eye, hey – that's nothing! It's amazing how your perspective changes. You know that saying, 'In the land of the blind, the one-eyed man is king'?

For the first six months after I lost my eye, my brain kept telling me I could see something that wasn't there. That's not unusual. It's like when someone has their arm cut off, they still feel things in their hand, although the hand isn't there. It's the same with the eye: the brain thinks that you're seeing something through that eye, even though it's not there. I call it 'ghosting'. The way that I stopped the ghosting was to cover that eye. I'd put my hand over my eye, and then my brain would know that I couldn't see out of that eye. It only lasted six months or so. I don't get it now, but I still have this habit of covering my left eye – a hangover from those first six months.

Someone said to me the other day, on learning that I only have one eye, 'Your eye looks really good! Do you notice that you don't have an eye?'

I said to him, 'Do you notice that you've got an arm?'

He was a bit taken aback by that. 'Well, no, not really, you just take it for granted.'

'Well,' I said, 'when you lose an eye, it's pretty much the same.'

He didn't have anything to say after that.

Actually, losing an eye isn't really the same as losing an arm. I guess if you're going to lose an organ, an eye probably has less impact than others. We've got two of them, for a start.

I still drive – badly. I've got scratches all over my car and I'm planning to sell it. When I got this diagnosis in November 2014, I bought myself an expensive Audi four-wheel drive which soon accumulated a whole lot of scratches because my distance vision isn't so good. Jacqui tells me that my parking was terrible even before I lost the eye!

My squash wasn't so good after losing the eye, either, although I went on playing for as long as I could. One time when I was at the ocularist – that's the person who made my artificial eye – I noticed that the other person seated in the waiting room also had only one eye.

When I went in, I asked the ocularist, 'So, the guy in the waiting room… What happened to him? Has he got what I've got?'

'No,' she replied. 'He lost his eye from being hit by a squash ball.'

Since then, I've always worn safety goggles playing squash.

When you're facing mortality eyeball to eyeball, so to speak, it certainly brings things very sharply into focus – pardon the puns! I think I forgive myself more for making mistakes. It might have something to do with being a middle child, but I've always had a desire to get along with everyone. I think getting on with different people is one of the things I'm good at; it's something I learned to do when I was young. I'm not sure I need to be liked by many people; I like being liked, but it's not such a big concern in my life that I've tried to avoid conflict, especially as I've got older. I think I avoided conflict when I was younger, like in my first marriage, but since then I've learned that avoiding conflict doesn't work. You can never avoid it, you can only delay it. Delaying conflict means a small issue festers and becomes a large issue, so I've learned to deal with things earlier.

I have this thing with Jacqui where I'll wake her up and say to her, 'Okay, what's the score?' – not necessarily because I think there might be a problem. It might be just to talk about how she thinks things are going. Sometimes it's just to test the water. I'll ask her, 'Where d'you think our relationship is at? What would you give it, out of ten? Is it seven or eight, or is it five or six?' It's never been less than five, as far as I can remember.

I learned to do that from my relationship with my first wife. We never dealt with issues when they arose. We'd wait until something exploded. Jacqui and I don't argue a lot, and I think it's partly because we deal with conflicts very early on. I've also been more direct, and said 'no' much more, since the diagnosis. I've been more upfront about my own needs than previously. So there have been changes. But the day-to-day stuff…it's all still the same. The point is that after the initial shock wears off, you've still got to get on with life.

One of the consequences of being told you only have a year to live is that you feel you need to rush everything. At the same time, you want to savour everything. When I first got the diagnosis, I just felt panic, disbelief, a sense of unreality – this couldn't be happening to me. It was all quite surreal. I didn't want to tell anyone at first, because that would make it real. When I did start telling people, beyond family and close friends, some of their reactions were telling. I got on the phone and told people, 'Things aren't looking so good. My cancer's metastasised.' Some people couldn't handle it. One guy put the phone down. We didn't know each other well, so maybe I was overstepping the bounds of our relationship by telling him that my cancer had metastasised and that it had no cure. But he actually hung up. He couldn't handle just how confrontational it was. And a number of people cried. You know that brilliant book, *Shantaram*? Kara, one of the main characters in *Shantaram*, says 'the truth is a bully we all pretend to like'. It's true. The truth for me is having a terminal illness. Faced with that truth, some of the people I've told have cried. It seemed to me that they cried not for me, but for themselves. I guess they were afraid and they couldn't cope with being forced to face mortality. I had that happen a number of times. People react in different ways – one could say in strange ways.

But most people have been wonderful. I've needed a lot of lifts to and from hospital over the last couple of years, and visitors to distract me when I have been hospitalised for days or weeks at a time. Every one of my mates has stepped forward to help. Being told I only had limited time also brought me closer to some special people. My friend Phil Jennings, for example, comes over to my house on Friday mornings to go for a walk or have breakfast with me before he goes to work. He's done that almost every Friday for the last three years. Another friend, Gordon Cairns, committed himself to coming to see me at home every month, in spite of his incredibly busy work schedule. If I go into the city, I know that no matter how busy my mate Angus Stewart is (he's a busy barrister), he'll drop everything to have a coffee with me. Gus Moors phones me once a week to find out how I am doing. Brett Hawkeswood is around at our place often, barbecuing and helping us to keep things together. We're incredibly lucky to have a group of such close friends in Sydney who have given us so much support over the last few years.

The family has been a huge help. Jacqui's brother Bruce, and his wife Lyn, are always there for us, practically and emotionally. When I was following a special diet, Lyn came and cooked up a storm for me every week. My older brother, Mark, who lives in Brisbane, has flown down to visit me every couple of months since my diagnosis. He's agreed to help Jacqui manage our financial affairs when I am gone. We've had to have some tough discussions about what will happen when I am no longer around.

My younger brother, Jonathan, lives in England, so I don't see him as often, but he and I have visited each other more over the last few years than we did before my diagnosis.

When I was first diagnosed, the staff and volunteers of Good Return each sent me a card with a personal message inside. There would have been more than forty cards, and I still have every one of them.

∞

After the cancer metastasised, I told the people closest to me that I'd been given a year. That was over three years ago. In that time, I've worked, I've travelled, I've kissed my wife, hugged my children. I've looked out of my study window at home and seen the leaves on the trees beside our driveway turn bright red in the autumn. I appreciate that beautiful sight all the more for knowing I might never see it again.

Having a terminal illness brings greater clarity, but no greater understanding. No great insights. I heard someone say the other day it brings the distinction, but it doesn't make a difference, ultimately. I think that's right. The understanding I had before I was told I had terminal cancer was no different after the shock had worn off. I didn't gain some great insight into life, other than that it's precious. And it's in short supply.

∞

Guy tells me that Jacqui's father, who's had a serious heart condition for a few years, is due to go into hospital in a couple of days for a procedure that will – hopefully – kick-start his heart and shock it into recalibrating.

Guy and I were due to talk on Sunday that same week. Neither of us could find a spare morning before then; it had been a busy week for both of us. Then, on Friday night, while idly trawling through the dross that makes up most of the posts on Facebook, I saw a photo of Jacqui and her dad at her graduation – smiling at the camera, pleased as punch. Her dad looked really proud. I wondered why she'd posted the photo. Was it the anniversary of her graduation?

A few posts further down, I read the devastating news: Jacqui's father had died. I knew they were very close. Her parents had lived with them and their growing family since they'd moved to Australia, soon after Guy and Jacqui had immigrated.

Guy and Jacqui took themselves off to the Blue Mountains the following weekend. On 30 June 2017 Jacqui posted on Facebook:

'I am looking out across the Blue Mountains again this year, my dad and Tim [Jacqui's brother] both very much in my heart. Will be raising a glass of whiskey tonight...'

And below a photo of Tim, sitting cross-legged on a banana lounge in his English backyard, surrounded by gift-wrapped packages, was a second post, this one from 2016:

'Thinking of my dear brother Tim today on what would have been his 56th birthday. So grateful that we got to spend this day with him last year, showering him with love and gifts...'

A memorial wake for David Savage, Jacqui's father, was held on 8 July at their home in Sydney. Despite the sadness, the wake was – as Jacqui put it – for celebrating and honouring a life so well lived.

∞

David and Joliette, Jacqui's parents, emigrated from South Africa to Australia soon after we made the move in early 2002. David had his seventieth birthday not long after they came to live with us. We had a birthday party for him at home. He gave a speech on our deck, and he said something that I've always remembered – something that's especially relevant now: 'Happiness is a decision.' From my own perspective, getting back up on your feet after a fall, metaphorically speaking, is a decision. You make the decision to be happy. It's one of the best pieces of advice I've ever heard. David was a very positive guy. I don't just admire that; I love it. I want to echo it in my own life. He was also quite stoic. He was in a lot of pain in his last six months, with cancer and back problems and so on.

The house is a lot emptier now that David is gone. It's his presence that I miss, even more than when my own father died in South Africa, six years ago, because I hadn't lived with my parents for many years. David helped us in so many practical ways. In the early years after we emigrated, I was away for a huge amount of time, travelling for work. Without David and Joliette, it would've been impossible. They looked after the kids, and they supported Jacqui, practically and emotionally.

I told David last year how much I appreciated their support.

He brushed it off in a very matter-of-fact way. He said something like 'That's good to know', and left it at that.

He wasn't a demonstrative sort of person. He was obviously of another generation and wouldn't talk about his feelings as much. Clearly he adored Jacqui and loved his grandkids, but he'd give the dogs more overt affection than he would anyone else! I'm much more of a heart-on-my-sleeve sort of person – much more demonstrative, more emotional. More passionate, more vehement. It's not all positive, in other words! Often it is, but I also have many downs amongst the ups.

David's death has left a hole, a physical hole. I miss his presence in the house. His illness and death at home have left me wondering… Towards the end, if I need a lot of care, would going into a hospice be easier on the family?

# 4

# 'Toilet Guy!'

*'A good head and a good heart are always a formidable combination'* – Nelson Mandela

Nineteen-eighty-nine was the year that the South African government announced the release of Nelson Mandela. That was the year that my first marriage fell apart. I was twenty-seven; I'd finished my master's degree at the end of the previous year and had started looking for work. I needed to pay off a few loans, so getting a job was a top priority. I applied for a couple of positions: one with a town planning consultancy, and the other with a development bank, the KwaZulu Finance and Investment Corporation. Later it changed its name to the Ithala Development and Finance Corporation. The bank's aim and mission were to provide economic development to black South Africans in the province of KwaZulu.

I was offered both jobs, but what attracted me to the job with the development bank was the link between finance and infrastructure. I had a degree in commerce as well as the master's in town planning, and the job combined the two. I was also attracted to the community development nature of the role. I'd be working in the bank's training outreach program. I wanted a job that gave me independence, and in my interview with the development bank it was clear that I'd have a lot of autonomy. The job with the town planning consulting company offered more money, but it was clear that I'd be at the beck and call of clients, and I'd have had far less independence.

I started work at the KwaZulu Finance and Investment Corporation in February 1989 and stayed there for about three years. It was a fairly big organisation with two or three thousand staff. The department I was in, the Training Trust, had about two hundred staff, and I was appointed to run the community development section within the Training Trust. Our role was to build community infrastructure – community libraries, community learning centres, water projects, roads – with funds from the development bank. The Training Trust either borrowed the funds from the bank under an internal arrangement, or the bank would lend to a local government council – a regional services council, like a municipal council, but in a rural area, and the council would generally contract us to manage the project.

The KwaZulu Finance and Investment Corporation had been set up to help develop what was then part of the apartheid state, the Bantustan of KwaZulu, through what was then called a 'homeland' government. From around 1976, this homeland government was led by Chief Mangosuthu ('Gatsha') Buthelezi. He held the position of chief minister until 2004. Politically speaking, the KwaZulu Finance and Investment Corporation was associated with Chief Minister Gatsha Buthelezi and his Zulu-aligned Inkatha Freedom Party. His cabinet appointed the board of the corporation, but it was run as a non-profit 'quango' (quasi-autonomous non-government organisation), so while the board of directors was appointed by the government, it operated independently.

As an ANC member, I was in effect politically opposed to the corporation's affiliation with the government. The ANC's support base was quite broad and included some educated urban Zulus, but its roots originally were with the Xhosa, which is an entirely different ethnic group. Buthelezi exploited these tribal and ethnic differences to drive a wedge between them. He created conflict; he used ethnicity to set one group against another. By branding himself as the head of the 'Zulu party', he was saying, in effect, 'If you support the Zulus, you're with me. If you support the Xhosa, then you're against me.' At that time, six to eight million people identified themselves as Zulus. Even today, Zulus are the single largest ethnic minority in South Africa. If Buthelezi had succeeded in getting the majority of Zulus on his side, it would've constituted a significant voting bloc. People assumed that if you were Zulu then you supported Buthelezi, but that wasn't true. A lot of urban Zulus – including many of my Zulu friends – supported the ANC.

Although I didn't like the idea of working for a corporation set up by the apartheid state and associated with Buthelezi's government, I believed the work itself was important. We were working in townships and rural areas, building infrastructure for use by the local community. The bank had a fairly good reputation at that time. There wasn't a high level of corruption then, and within the constraints of what the government was able to do, they did the best work they could.

The section I worked in also provided vocational training to local people to give them skills so they could work on these construction projects. They learned to become bricklayers, carpenters and motor mechanics, working on projects in their own community. That was really good: it gave them jobs and income. It also gave them a sense of ownership over the project in their community, a sense of pride. It was during this time that I came to believe that providing people with opportunities for meaningful work is surely one of the best and most sustainable ways of achieving positive social justice outcomes.

One project we worked on was in Folweni, a township outside Durban. The infrastructure in the township was extremely basic: there were virtually no amenities, no sewerage system. We worked with local communities to plan and build a community hall and learning centre, and to improve the sanitation. I helped to have two thousand pit latrines installed – earning me the nickname 'Toilet Guy'!

I learned a lot about infrastructure and about working with communities and with local government while I was with the development bank. A lot of what we were doing was good and genuinely helped to improve people's living conditions, but over time I came to realise how much politics played a role in decisions about where and how we worked. That wasn't so good. There was a big road project up in the Drakensburg mountains that I worked on, a few hundred kilometres west of Durban. The project involved working in a small community, tarring a dirt road round a dam. There were two roads around the dam: one went closer to the dam, and the other went further out. We undertook comprehensive technical assessments, looking at the feasibility of each road from an environmental, engineering and economic perspective. Then we talked with the community about their needs and priorities and how improving the road would help them. We asked them which of the two roads they wanted to have tarred. The community made a choice, and on that basis we made our recommendation. But the politicians and this homeland quango that I was working for wanted to tar the other road. So instead of doing what was best for the community and what the community wanted, what actually happened was based on an entirely different agenda. We had no power. That was part of the reason I eventually chose to move on.

While I was working there, about fifteen of the staff got together and set up a stokvel, a community savings group. We'd get together and contribute savings regularly. If someone wanted to borrow some money, then they'd pay a high interest rate, and we'd share the interest amongst us all. We would also share the management of the stokvel. We'd each take the role of treasurer for a month, sharing the responsibility of looking after the savings, calculating how much money each person put in and so on. What we were doing was essentially microfinance – but it was all done on a handshake. I guess we trusted each other. Too much, it turned out. One of the members was a young guy named Fortune, ironically. He had a round face and a friendly smile. When it came to his turn to take on the role of treasurer, he ran away with the lot – the crook! I lost 900 rand, about $90 in today's terms. But in those days, nearly thirty years ago, it would've been worth about $500. I definitely felt it. The other people in the savings group were pretty pissed off. If they'd have got their hands on him, I think they might've killed him. I didn't want to get involved. Fortune must've known what they might do, because he actually left the country.

∞

In 1992, after the ANC was unbanned, many exiled ANC members started returning to South Africa. Some had left the country to become members of the armed wing of the ANC, and a few had left because they didn't want to do military service. South Africans were in exile all over the world.

Many of these returning exiles didn't have much education, and they were coming back to South Africa without jobs or skills. A small group of people with very strong ANC connections started an organisation to provide training and skills for these exiles. It was called Khuphuka, which in Zulu means 'go up'. If you get into a lift in Durban, or in other parts of the country where people speak Zulu, you'll hear people say, 'Ukukhuphuka?', meaning 'Do you want to go up?' Khuphuka was looking for an operations manager. The organisation was only just starting up at that time; it was still very small, with just a handful of staff. Its leader was Stelios Comninos, an ANC member who had himself been living in exile in Zimbabwe. Neither he nor the other staff – all of them returning exiles – were familiar with the local legislation, the process of registration as a non-profit organisation, the learning methodologies that were approved by the training regulatory agencies. They needed someone who knew all about that stuff. In terms of skills, I ticked all the boxes.

Towards the end of my interview, Stelios said to me, 'So, you're currently working for the KwaZula Finance and Investment Corporation, that apartheid state organisation. What's the story?'

'Well,' I said, 'I needed a job!'

'All of us here in Khuphuka were in exile with the ANC,' said Stelios. As far as they were concerned, I had been working for the 'other side'.

'I'm a member of the ANC myself,' I replied.

Stelios was sceptical. 'Oh yeah?' he said. 'I'll check it out.'

He told me later that he'd contacted the local branch and found that I was telling the truth. I'm sure being a member of the ANC helped me get the job; it wasn't essential, but with the ANC on the verge of civil war with the Inkatha Freedom Party, it was important to demonstrate that I wasn't aligned with Inkatha.

Stelios was very closely connected within the ANC; he was a member of the armed wing, known as Umkhonto we Sziwe (Spear of the Nation), and treasurer of the Durban central branch of the ANC until the 1994 elections. He had been quite vocal before he went into exile, which would have been one of the main reasons why he didn't return to South Africa until 1991. One great advantage of this was that he had many valuable connections, some of whom joined the board of Khuphuka.

∞

I joined Khuphuka in 1992 as the operations manager to help put their programs in place. Our approach was to employ local people as unskilled labourers to work on civil infrastructure projects in their own communities. But what was really needed was skilled labour, so we began training local people in building and construction work and then employed them on projects in their communities. In that sense, the work followed a similar approach to the KwaZulu development bank, where we trained local people in the skills needed to work on improving their communities' infrastructure.

We grew the organisation rapidly. Over the next five years, we recruited six hundred staff and trainees and developed into a training-with-production organisation, training people in bricklaying, tiling, carpentry, plumbing, roofing, electrical – those kinds of skills. We'd tender on projects with municipalities, undertaking to employ as many members of the local community as we could. We'd employ skilled artisans who'd lead the teams of local community members that we'd trained. In the context of the widespread poverty and lack of infrastructure in many communities, what we were doing was incredibly important. We were giving people skills. We were giving them jobs. We were giving them a way to earn a living in the longer term and improve their lives, and our approach of training and employing local people enabled the municipalities to gain access to those communities at a time when violence often made that very difficult. We won quite a few projects on that basis. It was a really great program.

I'd learned a lot while I was working at the Training Trust in the KwaZulu Finance and Investment Corporation. I'd learned a lot about the technical aspects of adult learning and the theoretical aspects of andragogy – the principles and methods around how adults learn. I took courses on competency-based learning methodologies and modular learning methodologies, and this training was highly relevant to my work with Khuphuka. It was with Khuphuka that I had the opportunity to apply the theory in practice and learn from that experience.

As part of my work with Khuphuka, I had been giving advice to the trade union movement on the national education standards. Some of the trade unionists were on the board of Phambili High School, a school in Durban that had been established a few years before. It was known in the media as a very progressive school associated with the liberation movement. Most of the students were drawn from poor communities; many were the children of trade unionists. When the ANC was unbanned in South Africa, a lot of returning exiles sent their kids to Phambili High School. Some of the board members and parents whose children were attending the school asked me if I could come and help out. I can't remember exactly how it happened, but I got invited to join the board, and then after a couple of years I was elected as the chair. I became very involved in the day-to-day management of the school, and the principal, Robin Stuart, became a good friend. We often discussed school matters late into the evening.

Working with Khuphuka taught me the value of having a powerful board. Strong governance was incredibly important, and with his great political connections, Stelios was able to attract powerful people onto the board, many of whom have gone on to become leaders and senior politicians. Nkosazana Zuma, for example, was minister of health from 1994 to '99 under Nelson Mandela, then minister of foreign

*Guy with Obed Mlaba, South African High Commission, London, 1996.*

affairs under Thabo Mbeki and Kgalema Motlanthe. Nkosazana then became the first woman to chair the African Union Commission, a position she held up until the end of January 2017. Another Khuphuka board member, Duncan Hindle, became the director-general of South Africa's Department of Education, and Richard Lister was a Truth and Reconciliation Commissioner in the 90s.

Another member of the board was Obed Mlaba, who was elected as the first mayor of Durban after the transition to democracy, and later was appointed as the high commissioner of South Africa in the UK until September 2017. Obed and I became good mates when we travelled to Geneva together on a UN-sponsored trip to visit the International Labor Organisation (ILO). Our trip to the ILO was to learn about training methodologies, particularly around small business development. I couldn't believe how expensive Geneva was. We received a per diem, but the hotels were so expensive that he and I shared a room. We stayed in Geneva for about ten days and finished a day earlier than planned, so then we decided to spend a day in London. Obed had never been to London before and I was determined to show him everything. London in just twenty hours!

'I'm taking you everywhere,' I told him. And I did. I'd stand him in front of Buckingham Palace, or the Houses of Parliament, or whatever, and take his picture, and then we'd grab a taxi and race on.

'Wow, this is great!' he'd say, gazing out of the taxi window as Piccadilly Circus or Hyde Park whizzed by.

I gave him five minutes to watch the Changing of the Guard. Five more minutes in Trafalgar Square.

Outside Harrods, he said, 'Let's go in – I want to do some shopping.'

'No time for shopping!' I told him. 'We've still got more places to see!'

We had one day, and we did it all. It was crazy – quite hilarious! We were completely exhausted by the time we got on the plane. And to think that twenty years later he'd be living in London as high commissioner to the UK!

∞

I worked at Khuphuka for five years. We were doing good work, but over time I learned that it wasn't enough. Training local people as carpenters, tilers or plumbers and employing them for a while to build a road or a community hall didn't guarantee them a future. Once that project was finished, we'd move on to the next project in the next community. We couldn't employ the same people who'd been working on the previous project; we were obliged to hire and train local people from the next community we were working in. Over those five years, we kept training new people and employing them to work on their own community project, and when that project was finished, we'd move on. Some of the people we'd trained were able to get other work – road maintenance and other building work, that kind of thing – so they were able to go on using the skills that we had trained them in. But not everyone. Some tried setting themselves up in business, like small building and construction enterprises, but they often failed. The problem was that many of them had the practical skills, but not the business skills. People who are good at bricklaying aren't necessarily good business people! We realised that they needed training in different skills. That was when Obed and I went to Geneva, to learn about training methodologies for small business development.

Following that trip, Khuphuka started providing some support in that area, teaching people the skills to set up and run small businesses. But we only had limited success. One of the obstacles was performance bonds, which are required for many building and infrastructure projects, in case for any reason the project doesn't get completed. On a project worth a million rand, for example – the equivalent of $100,000 today – you'd usually need to provide a performance bond of about five per cent. That's 50,000 rand; roughly $5,000. Of course, the people we were working with came from very poor communities and simply didn't have that sort of capital. They started asking us for loans to cover their performance bonds. We provided one or two. Then we lost one performance bond and we learned our lesson. We just weren't in the lending game.

The answer seemed to me to be to develop a division of Khuphuka as a financial services institution. I wanted to help poor people build up their capital through savings and get them started in small business enterprises by providing them with low-interest loans. I'd had a bit of experience in lending, mainly from my work with the KwaZula Finance and Investment Corporation, and I put together a proposal to set up a microfinance institution and presented it to the board of Khuphuka. Stelios wasn't convinced, and the board's response was lukewarm: 'We've grown very rapidly in recent years. We're trying to do too many things too fast. Let's just focus.' Stelios agreed, and I guess I did too. Khuphuka wasn't yet ready to move into microfinance.

∞

One great advantage of having a board with strong political connections was that we had no problem raising funds. The European Union was by far our biggest funder: they gave us around 26,000,000 euros over five years. We also got funds from the US government, although some of our board members were less keen on that. Many of us felt strongly that we should not accept money from the World Bank. Loans from the World Bank and the International Monetary Fund, and even the International Finance Corporation to some degree, come with conditions. These institutions provide loans to developing countries in exchange for control. Taking a loan from the World Bank means you have to agree to implement major reforms – 'structural adjustments', they're known as – which often include drastically reducing your public sector. In some countries, that has meant getting rid of a huge number of government staff. That's what happened when the World Bank lent money to countries like Zambia or Tanzania. They provided huge loans on condition that they implemented certain reforms and balanced their budgets. It wasn't so much the policies themselves that we objected to; it was handing over control of your country to a bunch of international technocrats. After fighting for seventy years to get control of your country, to finally achieve democracy, that just didn't sit well. We were very proud of what we'd achieved. It was an amazing time. The people had voted in the ANC government, with Nelson Mandela as president. We were euphoric. We were deeply committed to the country's development. I had high hopes for South Africa at that time.

∞

Around the same time, I succeeded in getting support from a USAID project to go to the United States for a couple of weeks to study small business development. USAID funded the project, but it was managed by World Education in America. While I was over there, I visited the World Education headquarters in Boston and met up with some of the staff. I also met with a number of small business development corporations and community development corporations.

In the US, banks are required to lend a certain amount to help people in need. One way the banks do this is by funding small community development projects, often through community investment corporations. While I was over there, I met up with one of these community investment corporations – Coastal Enterprises Incorporated, based in Maine. The following year I went back there for an internship, learning more about lending for small business. I spent a month or two there, and over that time I solidified my friendship with a number of the World Education staff in Boston, especially a former South African, Gill Garb, who is still a close friend.

Then in 1997 a project came up, funded by USAID. The Ntinga Micro-Enterprise Program was designed to work with nascent microfinance institutions in South Africa, helping them to provide microfinance and lending services to support the development of small enterprises. World Education wanted to put in a bid, but they weren't operating in South Africa, so they put in a bid as the lead organisation in a consortium made up of two microfinance banks, the Kenya Rural Enterprise Program and the Rural Finance Facility, based in Johannesburg, with Khuphuka as the fourth consortium partner.

We won the project. It was a big win: the project was worth around US$3.5 million, to be spent over three years. The proposed project director, or chief of party as the position is called by USAID, was a very bright and capable woman on the staff of Khuphuka, Ntsuntsu Mahlungu. She had worked with Jacqui for a while before joining Khuphuka and was a good friend of ours.

A month before the project was due to start, Ntsuntsu came into my office to tell me she had changed her mind about the position. 'I'm sorry about this, Guy,' she said, 'but I've been offered a really good job with the South African Railway Corporation, with a lot of responsibility. This is a huge opportunity for me.'

World Education then had to find a replacement for Ntsuntsu.

A few days later, I got a call from Gill Garb, who was to be the World Education project manager based in Boston. She said, 'Guy, you worked for a development bank. You've got a degree in business finance, and you've been working in small business development. Why don't we put your name forward as the project director?'

It was an incredible opportunity. In fact, I was well qualified for the job: I'd been giving advice to the trade union movement on new training institutions, in the restructuring of the training industry and the national qualifications framework in South Africa, including in enterprise development and small business development.

I went to Stelios and told him about the offer. I was ready for a change; I'd been working with Khuphuka for five years. I wanted to get into microfinance. More importantly, I wanted to run my own show. I told Stelios that I wanted to be seconded to the USAID project.

He was supportive, as was the board, but he said, 'You say you want to be seconded, but you won't come back.'

He and the board gave me their blessing, but he was right; I didn't go back.

∞

The last time I saw Stelios was when I was visiting South Africa in 2014, just after my mother died. We met up over a coffee and inevitably started discussing politics. Stelios was deeply disillusioned with the ANC, the party he had dedicated so much of his life to. He didn't talk about the reasons for his disillusionment, but corruption in the leadership must have been a major factor. Jacob Zuma was serving his second term of office as president. He'd been charged with rape and had actually said under oath that he'd taken a shower after sex so that he wouldn't catch AIDS. He had persuaded the government to give him something like 250 million rand – around $26 million – to build him a house. He said he needed the money to install security systems, but in fact he built a huge luxury mansion with a swimming pool. As president, I didn't think it would be possible to prosecute him for corruption. If anyone in his cabinet spoke up against him, he'd just get rid of them. The corruption reinforced my decision to leave South Africa.

Nkosazana Zuma, the former health minister who was on the board of Khuphuka, was Jacob Zuma's second wife until they divorced in 1998. She visited me in Uganda, when I was working there, while she was on an official visit as foreign minister. She came to see me for a couple of hours and greeted me with a big hug. She gave me a hard time, though. I was the head of a microfinance bank in Uganda at that time, and she claimed that microfinance was just ripping off poor people. We had a bit of an argument about that. She agreed savings and insurance were good but loans, no; poor people shouldn't have to take loans, because debt can impoverish them further. That's true, and it would be great if there was enough money to hand out to people. But there isn't, and cash handouts aren't necessarily a good thing. There are social welfare projects, of course: payment transfers, they're called. In fact, I've been involved in projects in Bangladesh and Laos that have involved payment transfers. People receive cash, seeds and other assets. The problem is that payment transfers aren't sustainable and can't be scaled up. For the $3,000,000 we spent in cash handouts, we were able to help about six hundred families, whereas for the same amount of money we would've been able to give out loans sustainably to tens of thousands of people.

I don't know if Stelios still has his ANC membership card. I still have mine, but I have no real belief in the ANC now. About ten or twelve years after South Africa became a democracy, the Nationalist Party merged with the ANC. It was around incorporation, in the Marxian sense: put simply, it's around keeping your friends close and your enemies closer. It's better to have them inside the tent pushing out, than have them outside the tent pushing in. It just showed how far the ANC liberation movement had bent its principles that they could merge with the party they'd fought so hard against for so many years. And how the Nationalist Party – the political party of apartheid – could bend their political values and beliefs, whatever they were, to such an extent that they could join the liberation party that they'd banned for forty or fifty years. Of course, I didn't support the Nationalist Party in any way, but I had thought that they actually believed the things they espoused. Clearly it was just short-termism of the worst kind. That merger, for me, was a big watershed. The idea that the party I'd supported for years would go to bed with the enemy... It was inconceivable. I felt shattered – like I was the only person marching to the sound of my own drum. Everyone else was marching to a different drum. They were in step and I was out. That's what it felt like.

∞

Migration is driven by pull factors and push factors. The crime rate in South Africa in the late 1990s was horrifying: there were about thirty thousand reported murders a year. One time when Jacqui was down at the beachfront she had been randomly punched in the kidneys by a young black guy. Our good friends Chris and Claire Hock had their home broken into when Claire was eight months pregnant. The guys who broke in told her, 'We won't hurt you – we're not going to rape you', and indeed she wasn't shot or raped. Everyone thought she'd been very lucky! Subsequently she and Chris were held up and shot at just outside their front gate by a couple of armed youths. A bullet just missed Claire's head – and again some of their friends' response was, 'Gee, how lucky are you!'

Around the time we were starting to think about leaving South Africa, we were living in a big old Victorian house on a corner block. One Saturday morning, the year before we left, a car drew up at a stop sign outside our house and two young guys rushed up to the car and tried to hijack it. I heard later that the driver was a policeman. Maybe he was or maybe he wasn't, I don't know, but either way it makes no difference. He pulled out a gun and shot them both. I heard the gunshots and rushed outside into the street. There was blood everywhere – you wouldn't believe how much blood – pouring down the gutter. Someone called an ambulance, but I think one of the men was already dead. Later, Jacqui and I had to go out. As we backed down the driveway, I saw there was still blood on the road and in the gutter.

We didn't have kids then, but the idea of bringing up a family in that situation, with things being so unstable politically and the violence on our doorstep… No. It wasn't going to happen. It was just too much.

I was beginning to feel a growing sense of alienation, of not belonging. My involvement with the ANC and the liberation movement meant that I no longer felt part of the mainstream white community and, although I had many black friends, I didn't really feel part of the black community either. The push factors were mounting.

When we considered the options around our future and where we might live, we thought about the kind of life that many of our expat friends were living. A lot of them would stay a few years in one place and then move on. One Canadian couple we knew very well moved from the Philippines to Uganda, from Uganda to Switzerland, from Switzerland to Zambia, and then from Zambia back to Canada. Another couple from England, who were working for the British Department for International Development, lived in Uganda for two years and then moved back to England. Jacqui didn't want that life. She's a nester. I'm less of a nester; my home is where Jacqui and the kids are, I guess. For me, home could have been anywhere, but Jacqui was adamant; she just didn't want that nomadic lifestyle.

∞

We first visited Australia in about 1997, when we came to see my brother Mark in Brisbane and friends in Sydney. We had no intention of immigrating at that point. It was just a holiday. But a couple of things happened that led us to thinking about leaving South Africa for good and moving to Australia permanently.

The first thing happened when I went into a newsagent in Sydney to buy a newspaper. I picked up a copy of the *Sydney Morning Herald* – a paper that I'd never heard of before! – and on the front page there was a picture of some people chained to a tree. I glanced through the article and read that these people were protesting against the planned removal of trees in Centennial Park to get rid of the fruit bats that were living there. And I thought, where are the robberies and the murders? That's what was normally on the front page of the papers back home.

So I said to the guy selling the newspaper – and I cringe to think of it now – 'This is obviously your local paper. Can you give me a copy of your main paper?'

I was shocked when the man told me the *Herald* was one of the leading national papers. It brought home to me that things were very different in South Africa. It made me think again about the analogy of the frog in boiling water.

The second thing that happened was when we were visiting Avalon on Sydney's northern beaches. Just a month or so before we came on holiday to Australia, a branch of Barclays Bank in Durban had been robbed. A couple of people were shot and killed and a few others wounded. I happened to drive past in the morning, just after the robbery had taken place, and I saw them hosing down the pavement outside the bank. They cleaned the place up and then they reopened for business again at three in the afternoon. That's normal. If robberies and murders are commonplace, then work and life just have to carry on as usual.

So, there we were in Avalon, and I wanted to change some travellers' cheques. We stopped off at a bank. When I entered the bank, the first thing I noticed was the absence of security cages and barbed wire and an armed guard by the door. There were no double doors to go through, which are quite common in South Africa: you enter through the first door, and that door has to close before the second door will open. So I went into this bank at Avalon and it was all very open, and there was a woman standing by the front door next to a small table on which there was a large cake, cut into slices. A few slices had already been taken.

The woman smiled at me, gestured to the cake, and said, very pleasantly, 'Would you like a piece of cake?'

'Sure, thanks!' I said. 'What's the occasion?'

'We opened this branch today. It's our first day!'

Being me, I immediately got chatting with her. I said, 'That's great! So, you guys are expanding?'

'No, what actually happened was that we had a branch down the

*Winship family party to farewell Mark's move to Australia, 1995.
L to R: Guy, Mark, Allan ('Rusty') and Jonathan.*

road and it got broken into. Someone came in with a knife and held up one of the staff. It was terribly traumatic for everyone. They all needed counselling afterwards and they couldn't work there any more. We had to close that branch and move to new premises.'

I was stunned. I just looked at her. My first thought was, you guys are weird! Back home, a bank was robbed and two people were murdered and they just washed away the blood and were open again for business in the afternoon. And then it dawned on me: it's not you that's weird, it's me. After all those years of violence in South Africa, I'd become desensitised. We'd all just grown used to that level of violence. It came as a shock to me to realise that that wasn't normal, and that of course having a knife at your throat was enough for anyone to be traumatised. It was completely reasonable to close the branch and open a new one.

After that trip to Australia, Jacqui and I often discussed these two incidents. It seemed to us that Australia didn't have any crime! We even wondered, what's wrong with the place? And then we thought, maybe it's not Australia that's 'wrong'; maybe it's us; maybe it's South Africa.

Those were the push factors. My parents were actively encouraging us to emigrate, and Jacqui's parents were prepared to move with us. By 1999 we had decided we would leave South Africa, and we initiated the long process of applying for permanent residence in Australia.

∞

From 1997 through until October '99, I worked as the project director on the Ntinga Micro-Enterprise Program, managing the program, and also acting as the country director for World Education for part of the time. I learned a lot about microfinance during those years. I managed to get USAID to support me to go back to the United States to study the top microfinance program in the world, at the Economic Institute at the University of Colorado in Boulder. I went back to Boston a few times during this period to visit the World Education offices and get to know the staff better. I also helped the regional director of FINCA (Fighting Poverty with Microfinance and Social Enterprises – a non-profit microfinance organisation) with a plan to set up an office in South Africa.

When the Ntinga project came to an end in late 1999, World Education wanted me to stay on to focus on fundraising and building their program in South Africa, which would have included health, water supplies, sanitation, and various other development interventions. But I wasn't interested in fundraising; I wanted to keep working on microfinance.

At around the same time, I had applied for a job with Habitat for Humanity in Cape Town, heading up their South Africa office. They were looking for someone who had experience working at a senior level in the NGO sector, with a background in infrastructure and training. It was perfect for me. I had all the right skills and I had the political connections. Moving to Cape Town also had a lot of appeal. It's a lovely city in a beautiful wine-growing region, about two thousand kilometres from Durban on the other side of the continent.

The recruitment agency managing the process told me they were recommending me for the job.

Then I got a call from a woman at the agency. She said, 'Look, Guy, I'm afraid I just have to tell you, they're not going to appoint a white candidate.'

I said, 'Gee, that's not good news for me. Did they tell you that?'

'No, they haven't actually told me,' she said, 'but I know that's what they're going to do. I didn't want to tell you. It's unofficial, of course – but it's their choice. I'll deny it if you ask them.'

Of course, affirmative action was encoded in the law in post-apartheid South Africa. I had been outspoken in my support for affirmative action, specifically for black South Africans and for women, but I confess it didn't feel great when it affected me negatively. I was well aware of the irony, but at a personal level I wanted a job where I'd be valued for what I could offer and where I could make a meaningful contribution.

'So, what now?' I asked the woman from the recruitment agency.

She said, 'I know of a couple of other NGOs that are looking to fill senior positions. But they're not going to employ a white person either.'

I started looking around for other jobs outside South Africa. I saw an ad in the paper for a position with FINCA Uganda. They were advertising for the managing director and chief executive officer of FINCA Uganda, based in Kampala. I applied, and in early September 1999, following a telephone interview, I received a letter offering me the job.

# 5

# 'Rats ate my money!'

'If a free society cannot help the many who are poor, it cannot save the few who are rich' – John F. Kennedy

A few days before I was offered the job of heading up FINCA Uganda, Jacqui went into labour and gave birth to Thomas, our first child. He was seven weeks premature and weighed just under two kilos. He stayed in intensive care for two weeks before we could take him home, but he was back in hospital a few days later with severe jaundice. Initially it looked like he would need a blood transfusion, but to our relief this wasn't necessary in the end. They were pretty worrying, those early days of Thomas's life.

I first went to Uganda in October 1999, stayed for a month, and then went to the States for about two weeks to visit the FINCA headquarters in Washington. I flew back home to Durban for Christmas. At the beginning of January, Jacqui, Thomas and I all moved up to Kampala. Jacqui's mother Joliette joined us to lend Jacqui a hand; Thomas was just under four months old.

With a very young and seriously premature baby, Jacqui viewed the whole prospect of moving to Uganda as terrifying. Kampala is a bad malaria area, and Jacqui became a world expert on the habits of the female anopheles mosquito. When we arrived in Kampala, she was appalled to find there were no mosquito nets where we were staying, and she threatened to take Thomas and get on the next plane home. Her mother and I managed to persuade to talk her down, and the next day I organised a local carpenter to come and install hooks on the ceiling and put up nets. But we didn't take any chances: we started Thomas on antimalarial medicine right from the start.

By the time we moved to Uganda, the civil war had been over for about fifteen years and the country was enjoying greater peace and stability than it had known in decades. But the war had destroyed the economic base of the country. When Milton Obote resumed power in 1979, after the war between Tanzania and Uganda and during the civil war that followed, tens of thousands of people went missing – including the fathers and brothers of some of our staff at FINCA. They'd gone to the bus stop in the morning to catch the bus to work, and they'd never been seen again. No one ever knew what had happened to them. Many more people were killed when Milton Obote was in power than under Idi Amin. It was a terrible time. The impact on the Ugandan people was huge. I felt that the country was damaged psychologically as well as economically. Then, following the election in 1984, Yoweri Museveni became president, and by the time we arrived, the country had recovered to some extent: there was stability and the economy was growing. But the scars hadn't completely healed, and Uganda was still very poor. Yoweri Museveni was president while we were there and remains president today. Some say he'll stay president for life. Most people I spoke to during the time we lived there were happy to have him as president. They weren't so concerned about democracy; they just wanted stability and they wanted peace. After Idi Amin and Milton Obote, that was all people cared about.

∞

When I first joined FINCA at the end of 1999, it was running one of the largest microfinance programs in Africa, with nine branches around the country. By the time I left in 2002, there were around fourteen branches and about forty-five thousand loan clients.

We ran microfinance programs, mainly through village banks: groups of about thirty people, mostly women. A loans officer from

FINCA would go to a village and tell them about FINCA and about the services that they offered: loans, savings and insurance. If the villagers were interested, the loans officer would explain the rules around how they should establish a village bank: they should know the other people in the group; the group should meet regularly once a week or once a month, whenever best suited them; they should save a little bit of money to start with, and then pool their savings. They should also be interested in loans. Then the group would form, usually between twenty-five to thirty-five women. The group would elect a chair, a secretary and a treasurer, and then those people would receive two days of training. Not everyone was literate, so it was sometimes difficult finding someone to take on the role of secretary, but usually there'd be someone who could read and write enough to keep minutes of the meetings. Each person in the group would have a passbook in which their savings and loans would be recorded, and when the loans officer visited that group, they would check that the passbooks matched up with FINCA's bank records.

One of the first things I did when I got the job was to visit all the branches. Some were very remote: it could take eight hours or more to get there by road. You couldn't drive fast because the roads were so bad. I used to think that the roads were safer in Uganda because there were so many potholes you couldn't drive fast, and people would weave their way all over the place, trying to avoid the potholes. You could tell the people who were drunk, because they were the only ones who drove in a straight line!

Arua is a small town in north-west Uganda, about four hundred and eighty kilometres from Kampala. We established a branch of FINCA there; the American ambassador to Uganda came and opened the branch. Arua is one of the most remote and poorest places we worked in: less than an hour's drive to the border with South Sudan, and only about forty kilometres to the Congo border. FINCA had a social mission as well as a financial sustainability mission: we wanted to work with the poor. In remote areas like Arua, areas that are more prone to violence, people have far less access to financial services. We assessed the risks, and after careful consideration we decided that working up north near the border was a risk worth taking. The people in these very poor areas needed our services.

The first time I was due to visit Arua, a colleague and I had booked to fly there. The main domestic Ugandan airline at the time was Eagle Air. The day before we were due to fly, there was a picture of a plane crash splashed all over the front page of the newspaper – an Eagle Air plane at the airport in Arua! The report said that when the plane landed, the wheels just folded and the plane scraped along the runway on its undercarriage. I think everyone survived, but the plane was a mess. I wasn't taking any chances! I told the team, 'Hey, just scrap any plans for me to fly Eagle Air! I'm driving!' So I got the company car and a driver, and we drove the eight hours there.

While I was touring the northern part of the country, I also visited a couple of refugee camps. The conditions in the camps – like in most refugee camps all over the world – weren't great, but I guess they provided some protection. Most of the refugees were Somalis; there were some Congolese and Sudanese refugees as well. We were thinking about providing banking services to them, but the problem was that the Ugandan government didn't want those refugees to settle or get a job or start a business in Uganda because they could take jobs away from Ugandans, which may have been correct. They would've undercut the Ugandans because they were more desperate, frankly.

∞

Another branch I visited early on was in Masaka, a small town about one hundred and thirty kilometres south-west of Kampala. The equator crosses the southern part of Uganda, between Kampala and Masaka. Every time we drove down to the Masaka branch, when we reached the equator we'd all shout, 'This is the equator!' and we'd all jump out of the car and shake hands. We must've crossed the equator dozens of times, and we went through this crazy ritual every time. Anyway, I was visiting this branch in Masaka, meeting the staff and clients in the Masaka market. Getting to know your clients is a good thing to do for any bank; your clients are your key to success. Essentially we were operating a bank for poor people. The poor were our clients, and they were just as important to us as the clients of a big commercial bank are to that bank. It's one of the things I love about microfinance: you're not just providing a service to people and being paid by a third party, as is usually the case in most charities. You are providing services to people who know they are paying for your services – so you need to treat them as your clients, not just as recipients of the service. That really changes the power relationship.

In the Masaka market, about thirty local women had got together to form a savings group. This was just one of about a thousand such groups that FINCA Uganda was working with across the country. One of the women in the group – Audrey, I think her name was – ran a small business buying and selling cloth in the market. Audrey told me how important the savings services were to her. Her English wasn't too bad, so I was able to communicate directly with her rather than through an interpreter. Audrey said that before the savings scheme started, she kept her money in a tin. It was the only place she had where she thought she could keep her money safe. Then one day she looked in her tin – and found all the notes had gone! All that was left were a few shreds of paper. 'Rats!' she exclaimed, frowning with annoyance. 'Rats ate all my money!' I thought, how awful for that poor woman, discovering her hard-earned cash had disappeared. I guess the notes would've been well-used, grubby and worn…a tasty snack for a hungry rat!

If you're poor, you're highly vulnerable to economic shocks. You have much less capacity to deal with the unexpected, and not having access to savings services increases your vulnerability. Savings services help you to deal with those economic shocks by building up a buffer. Poor people are particularly vulnerable because even relatively small economic shocks can have a huge impact, and they have limited opportunities to earn income. Most have few employable skills. These factors increase both the likelihood of something going wrong with any particular venture, and the impact on a poor family if something does go wrong. Take farming, for example: there are always huge risks in farming, the kind of farming that millions of poor people engage in, especially if they depend on one main crop: they're at the mercy of the seasonal cycle, the rain, pests, the price of their produce. If a child gets sick, a poor family can go from being poor and just managing, to desperate – overnight. The fact that rats had eaten Audrey's money meant that her child's life might be at stake.

Banking is about trust. When a bank lends you money, they do a lot of checks on you: how much money you make, whether you have the capacity to repay, what are your assets and liabilities, whether you have someone who'll stand surety, whether you have collateral – all those kinds of things. Savings, on the other hand, is when you lend your money to the bank. And how do you know the bank is going to repay you? It's all about trust. I listened to Audrey talking about her trust in the group; how they built up their savings, and their trust in each other. She started off borrowing the equivalent of about $35. The group trusted her to make her repayments, and she in turn trusted her fellow members in the group to repay their loans, too. She told me how the savings had enabled her to build up a reserve, a protection for her family if and when things went bad.

∞

Soon after I started, we began the process of transforming FINCA Uganda from a non-profit organisation into a proper bank. That process involved applying for a full banking licence – a tier 3 or T3 banking licence – from the Central Bank. Without that licence, we were limited in what we could do: most importantly, we couldn't provide savings services directly until we were a regulated financial institution. Until we were granted a T3 banking licence, FINCA would facilitate bank accounts for the village microfinance groups with local banks, which were often located a long bus ride away in the nearest town.

I took on the process of applying for a full banking licence, and FINCA became the first microfinance institution in Uganda to be granted a T3 licence. It was also one of the few organisations in the world at that time that transformed from a non-profit credit institution to a licensed bank, a full profit savings and loans microfinance bank. That took a lot of work.

After getting the licence, FINCA was able to mobilise and manage its own savings programs. We also had a lot of people insured because we covered the families of people on loans. We had just under two hundred thousand people covered by life and accident insurance, as well as a few thousand on health insurance. I became known in the development sector for having succeeded in achieving that transformation. I guess that was one of the reasons I was in demand later for consulting work. After about six months, I was appointed to the board as managing director of FINCA Uganda.

∞

As a financial institution, we often needed to transport cash – either when we collected savings or when we distributed loans to our clients. We usually provided loans in cash, although occasionally we'd provide a cheque to a group and instruct the members to draw it at their local bank. That often wasn't practical, particularly when the local bank was an hour's bus ride away, so most of our loans were delivered in cash. Security was therefore extremely important. Petty theft was quite common, but we were lucky: we didn't have any major violent incidents. Whenever we transported money, an armed guard would accompany the staff in a four-wheel drive. We trained the staff in what to do and what not to do: there always had to be two people present in a delivery of cash; you had to change the routes; you weren't allowed to take the same route twice in a row. We reviewed the security of all the buildings, all the branch offices. We appointed security guards at each of the branches, twenty-four hours a day. We had safes installed, bolted to the floor in a locked room. We tightened up on internal controls. But in spite of all these safeguards, we did have a couple of cash-in-transit robberies. Of course, when a group was about to take delivery of a loan, it became common knowledge. Everyone got to know about it, which set us up for robberies. Secrecy was something the management felt was very important, but I knew that was impractical. How could you keep a cash delivery secret with thirty people knowing that they'll each be getting a $500 loan? They're bound to talk about it. Someone's bound to know.

Even though there were occasional robberies, none of the staff were seriously injured or killed, thankfully. Not much money was stolen in the few robberies that took place while I was there: $2,000 or $3,000, maybe. The amounts weren't huge. We had limits on how much cash could be disbursed at a time, so sometimes we'd split up the amount and make the disbursement in several lots over a couple of weeks. We had a lot of discussion around what was the best way of doing it, weighing up the risks of doing it one way or another: whether making the disbursement in two lots actually increased the risk, because then there were two chances of getting robbed instead of one.

We weren't the only ones who were at risk of being robbed. I remember a few stories about the women in the savings groups themselves being robbed – not only when they took out loans, but at other times, too. A lot of the women were dealing with cash every day as part of their businesses – growing and selling vegetables, for example, or cloth; women like Audrey. She'd sell her cloth and earn some cash, and then she'd have to find a safe place to store it until she could deposit it in a bank through the microfinance program. Husbands often resented their wives earning money. That was one of the biggest problems: husbands taking the money, sometimes with physical force. Sons, too – and occasionally daughters or mothers. I heard stories of sons and daughters stealing their mothers' hard-earned cash, usually in the middle of the night when everyone was asleep. They'd know where the money was stashed, and they'd take it and disappear. There were all kinds of incidents like that.

Husbands were a problem all the way through, at least on the business side. Not only with loans, but with any cash their wives earned; they would sometimes take it, if they could. We tried to support the women, to help them manage that risk. In our financial literacy programs, in our educational programs and in working with our partners, other NGOs, we'd try to provide education and skills to the women. Perhaps the most powerful way of dealing with this problem was by the women supporting each other as a group. I remember several incidents where a husband had become violent and beaten his wife and taken her money with physical force. The woman would tell the other members of her group, and together they would go to her house or to where the husband was working, and they would confront him as a group. They would say to him, 'What you did is wrong. You know this. It's not good for your family and it's not good for the community.' That worked more often than not. Working together, the women felt empowered – better able to confront a bullying husband.

Over time, we hoped we were making a difference in those communities by improving the women's status, both economically and socially.

∞

I enjoyed my time in Uganda. The work was great. FINCA was a big fish in a small pond, and a lot of people knew about us. We had adverts on the radio and in the newspapers. We'd go into a remote village and ask people there if they'd heard of us. 'FINCA?' they'd say. 'Yeah, yeah! We know who FINCA is!' I got a lot of satisfaction from knowing we were making a difference to the lives of many poor Ugandans.

The people of Uganda are called the Baganda, or Ganda, and

Luganda is their language. I tried to learn Luganda, but most of the people I knew and worked with spoke much better English than I would ever speak Luganda. They would speak English to each other because it's the official language – a legacy from Uganda's colonial history.

Uganda is a beautiful country, and Ugandans are incredibly warm and gentle people. There weren't the same racial tensions as there were in South Africa, with its history of apartheid. Even today, after twenty-five years of democracy and liberation, the racial tension is still palpable in South Africa. It's hard to make generalisations, but Kampala in 1999 was a much safer city than any town in South Africa. You could walk anywhere in Kampala, any time of the day or night.

But there were still violent episodes in some parts of the country, especially near the borders with Sudan and Congo. The Lord's Resistance Army guerrilla group was still very active at that time, luring or kidnapping young kids to join them. From the mid-80s to about 2009, they abducted tens of thousands of children – some as young as nine or ten – and made them serve as soldiers. Up until the time I started the job, FINCA had avoided working in those parts of the country where there was still violence. But the people in those areas desperately needed our services.

∞

Soon after I started at FINCA, I began to work on changing the culture of the organisation in subtle ways. We were having a Christmas party, and a cake had been cut up to share around. There's a tradition in Uganda that when there's food to share, like a cake, the boss would be offered a piece first, then the next piece would go to the next most senior person, and so on. The rest of the staff would receive their cake last – if there was any left! So at this Christmas party, the cake had been cut up and, following tradition, I was offered a piece of cake first. I wouldn't take it. I said, 'Hey, you eat first and I eat last. I work for

*Guy with colleagues at the FINCA Christmas function, Kampala, Uganda, 2000.*

you!' They took some persuading, but I insisted. There were grins and giggles all round. Later one of the managers came to my office and told me they'd never seen that before: a boss taking their share last. From then on, whenever we had an informal staff get-together where there was food, I made sure the staff would have theirs first and I would have mine last.

I also began to change some aspects of our organisational structure; the way in which we visualised it. Instead of having the managing director at the top, as most organisational charts have it, I inverted the triangle and put the MD at the bottom, and the managers above, and the rest of the staff above that. I wrote a memo to the staff saying, 'You work for the clients. We, the managers, work for you. Our job is to make sure you can do your job better. Your job is to make sure the clients do their job better.'

We started to introduce a whole range of new practices around client focus, client satisfaction, sales techniques. It's hard to steer the ship in a different direction – especially when the ship is an organisation with two hundred staff! – and I was constantly promoting the idea that we should put our clients first. It crystallised my thinking around who we were working for. We were working for the clients. Not for the government, not for a donor. I wanted to change the thinking about who we were working for and the way we worked.

One day I asked a couple of the field staff, 'Who do you work for?'

'We work for the branch manager,' they said.

'No,' I said. 'You don't. You work for the client. You work for those poor women.'

They looked confused. 'No, no, we work for the branch manager! We report to him.'

'Yes, you report to the branch manager – and he has to make sure that you're doing your work, and he must help you do your work. But you don't work for him. You don't work for him, and you don't work for me. You don't work for the funder. All of us work for the client. The poor.'

Then they nodded and said, 'Okay, yeah, you're right,' but they didn't change their behaviour. Not right away.

It took time and a huge amount of effort to make changes in people's thinking and in the organisational culture. I went on and on about it. I bored the team to death about it!

You can't train someone in an organisation's culture. Ultimately the way you change a culture is by the leadership setting an example, and other people in the organisation – the management and the staff who have been there longer – reflecting and mirroring and practising and living that culture. Culture is a lived practice. It's not enough to say that we are client-focused if in practice that isn't borne out.

One thing I learned in Uganda was how to bring about change in a way that was culturally appropriate and acceptable. From the time I started at FINCA in October 1999 until Christmas that year, I had a problem with meetings starting on time. Weekly management meetings were held on Monday mornings at nine o'clock, but people would drift in at five past, ten past nine – sometimes later. I went back to South Africa for Christmas, and when I returned in January, at our first meeting of the year I said to the staff, 'Okay, our next meeting will start at eight fifty-five.' I don't want to say that Ugandans are overly sensitive, but like in many other cultures, losing face is a big issue. You don't tell someone that they're not doing well in front of other people. I followed up that meeting with a memo saying that in future the management meetings will start at eight fifty-five. The operations manager put his head around my door and said, 'Hey, Guy, don't you mean nine o'clock?', and I said, 'No, I mean eight fifty-five.' What I meant was, of course, be punctual. And they all got the message. They understood. I wanted to do it in a culturally appropriate way. I racked my brains for a way to do it without getting annoyed or telling people they were late in front of others. Among the expats, there was this common perception that the local people were slack, that they were late for everything. Expats would talk about 'African time'. Some people even had these 'jokey' clocks that would go backwards. I didn't like any of that – not least because I too am African! My solution was to come up with a new start time: eight fifty-five. Some of the staff asked, 'Why eight fifty-five?', and I said, 'Well, we need to have five minutes to greet each other and ask each other how our weekend was. So we'll start at eight fifty-five, and then we can get onto business matters at nine.' It worked really well.

∞

On the personal side, things weren't going so well. There are always stresses and strains in moving to another country, and after the first year or so, Jacqui was bored; she was used to having a professional identity of her own, but in Uganda she couldn't get a work permit. She produced some training manuals while she was there, and she did a bit of psychotherapy consulting. Strictly speaking, it was illegal without a work permit, but a doctor we knew talked her into doing some counselling because there were so few psychologists in Kampala. She only did a small amount of work, but there was a problem. The expat community, who were her main client base, was just too small. She'd be counselling a client about their relationship difficulties, and then we'd meet them and their partner at a dinner party. Jacqui would be sitting there, knowing intimate details about their lives while having to engage in small talk. She found that very awkward.

∞

Uganda was great, but it was a bit of an expat life, I guess. There was a very small expat community – probably about eight thousand expats in the whole of Uganda. I felt like I was living two parallel lives – one, working to eradicate poverty, and the other, living in relative affluence with a maid, a gardener, a driver and a security guard. I remember waking early one morning and wandering into the kitchen to make myself a cup of coffee. It was warm, and I was stark naked – and I found myself face to face with the maid! I'm not sure which of us was the most surprised!

We also had a nanny for Thomas: Jane Birungi, a beautiful young Rwandan woman. Her parents had been Rwandan refugees; they had moved to Uganda just before the Rwandan genocide. Jane must've been twenty-two or twenty-three when she came to work with us. When we left Uganda, we got her a job with some friends in the British High Commission. They took her to England with them and she ended up migrating there. Later she got a job as a nanny with the family of the Rwandan ambassador, and from there she managed to get the right to work and live in England permanently. We've stayed in touch, and we're still in contact with her fifteen years on. In fact, we spent the day with her in London on our last visit to the UK in 2016.

Jane is an intelligent and competent person, but she just didn't have the opportunity to study. I think that's true of so many of the people that I work with. I don't want get into economic theory, but the reasons that poor people do some of the things they do are completely rational and intelligent. They might be uneducated and have dirt under their nails, but they certainly aren't stupid. They make rational decisions based on what they know. It's lack of knowledge, lack of education and lack of opportunity that keep them poor.

∞

A highlight of the expat year was the Ascot Goat Races. Everyone would get dressed up: it was Uganda's equivalent of the Melbourne Cup, I guess! It was a big annual fundraising event, and local businesses, shopkeepers, and big corporates would all support the races. The corporates would have their own tents, and you'd try and get invited to these tents. We put some money in and 'bought' a goat – well, we rented it, really, for the day. We called the goat Korsakoff Syndrome. In case you didn't know, Korsakoff Syndrome is the name of the condition one can get from repeated alcohol abuse: it's alcohol-related memory loss. Our goat Korsakoff Syndrome cost us about $100. It lived up to its name; it was a complete dope. It wandered around, bleating pathetically, and showed no interest in trying to get to the front of the flock. Jacqui described it as 'a dog of a goat'! Anyway, we had a lot of fun. Looking back, the whole event was pretty crazy, but some people took it very seriously. It was all part of the expat life in Uganda.

Jacqui and I went sailing regularly, and we'd go racing on Sunday afternoons. We had a laser, an Olympic-class dinghy, and we'd take turns to sail while one of us would look after Thomas. There were a couple of sailing clubs on Lake Victoria: one at Entebbe, about fifty kilometres south of Kampala, and the other at Kaazi, a little village close to Kampala. Once a year there'd be a big competition, sailing from Entebbe to Kaazi, which took all day. We'd sail through the Ssese Islands, a beautiful archipelago of little islands across the equator.

We were also members of the Kabira–Makindye Country Club, which is really quite a business, with a swimming pool and tennis courts. We'd go there regularly for dinner or at weekends. But Jacqui wasn't happy. As I said, she couldn't work. Most of the people she knew were the wives of men working in international development, or in the commercial sector. She used to say, 'If I have to go to one more ladies' tea party, I'll go crazy!' After about two years, she'd had enough. She was eager to move to Australia, although it took me another year to extricate myself. Things might have been different if she had been able to work.

∞

I talked earlier about the pull and push factors of migration. The politics, the corruption and the crime all reinforced our decision to leave South Africa. Jacqui's brother, Bruce, had come to Australia in 1998 to train a few members of the South African Olympic sailing team. He and his wife Lyn raved about Australia, and on the strength of that visit, they decided to emigrate.

When all's said and done, I guess the wealthy, stable country we were looking for seemed kind of tame after living in Africa. Maybe even boring! Australia is wealthy, it is stable, and I guess it is boring in some ways. It lacks the 'edge' of Africa, but we were more than ready to trade edge for safety and stability.

I feel some guilt about leaving South Africa. South Africa is a developing country, and I'm not there helping to develop it. That sounds arrogant, but to be honest, with my skills I could make a contribution – I could help the country rebuild, especially given that's the kind of work I've been doing for the past thirty years. And then there's also some guilt around the push factors, particularly the violence: leaving friends and remaining family members to face the music. Leaving your country is a bit like jumping ship. That's certainly how some fellow South Africans see it. You're leaving us. You're running away. You're a bit of a coward, avoiding responsibility. It didn't strike me as much then, when we emigrated, as it does now, but the level of corruption within the liberation movement – within the ANC, who are now in government – that was also a push factor. Some of the people who had been so critical of me twenty-five years ago – the people who had refused to see me or speak to me when they found out I supported the ANC – were especially critical of me leaving. And of course some of those people were worried about their own future in South Africa.

South Africa is my roots, but I've never felt a strong pull to go back and live there. I still have close friends there that I'd like to see more often, and there are some things that I miss: the Drakensberg mountains in the west of the province I grew up in, bordering Lesotho. They're quite spectacular; they rise steeply from the plain, with peaks up to eleven thousand feet. I went there many times, hiking and trekking. They hold a special place in my heart.

I missed my parents. I felt some guilt about not being there for them as they grew older. I tried to see them every year until they died. The only year I didn't go back was in 2013, when I lost my eye. My father had died by then, and my mom died in June the following year.

∞

By the time we were granted permanent residence visas and were able to move to Australia, I'd saved enough money to tide us over until I could find work. But even though money wasn't an immediate concern, there were a lot of unknowns, a lot of stresses and strains. The first morning after we arrived, I woke up in a sweat, wondering if we'd done the right thing. I lay there, my mind in turmoil. Was I ever going to find a job? Would our marriage survive? Would Australia ever be home for us?

# 6

# Starting over

'The journey of a thousand miles begins with one step' – Lao Tzu

Jacqui, Thomas and I arrived in Sydney on Australia Day, 26 January 2002. I'm not superstitious, but it seemed to me at the time that this was an auspicious start to our new life. Friends met us at the airport, waving WELCOME banners and balloons, and took us for a picnic at Balmoral, a beach facing the ocean on Sydney's northern side. It seemed that everyone in Australia was on holiday. In the blur of jet lag, it all felt a little surreal. One of the things that really startled me was the lack of black people. In Africa, wherever I was – but particularly in Uganda – I was surrounded by black people. In a crowd of a thousand people, I'd be the only white person. I didn't give it a second thought. But arriving in Sydney, one of the first things I noticed was that I couldn't see a single black person. That was a bit of shock to the system. The only things that felt familiar were the beaches and surfing and driving on the left side of the road.

FINCA had offered me a bonus to stay on in Uganda. I negotiated with them to continue for another six months, then wind things up, hand over to my replacement, and move to Australia permanently. So when we first arrived in Australia, I only stayed a week before going back to Uganda. During that week, Jacqui and I signed a lease on a house in Pymble – a suburb in Sydney's north-west – and bought a car. Jacqui started a job right away, teaching English as a second language. It had been too difficult to apply for psychology jobs in Australia while we were still in Uganda, but Jacqui was too anxious about our future not to have something lined up. In retrospect it was a crazy thing to do, but she set off for work in the city the morning after we flew in. A few weeks later, she succeeded in being offered a position as a psychologist, so her foray into ESL teaching was short-lived.

The next few months were hard for Jacqui and me. Back in Uganda, I spent a lot of time on my own, thinking about what I was going to do when I got to Australia. I applied half-heartedly for a few jobs – banking in emerging economies, that kind of thing – but I didn't have a lot of connections. The connections that I had were in international development organisations like the British Department for International Development (DFID), the German technical cooperation agency, GTZ, and UN agencies like the UN Capital Development Fund, related to the work I'd been doing.

FINCA flew me back to Australia at Easter so I could spend a week or so with the family. By then it was clear I'd been away too long, and after a couple more months in Uganda I wrapped things up with FINCA. When I arrived back in Sydney on 4 June 2002, I had a few assignments lined up with the World Bank, with GTZ, with the Central Bank of Indonesia and with various UN agencies, but I wasn't especially excited about the prospect of consulting work. It was interesting work, but it meant a lot of travelling. I didn't want to turn down any offers of assignments, so I was away a lot.

Not long after settling in Australia, I met with the two-person microfinance team (as it was then) in AusAID, the Australian government's aid agency before it merged with the Department of Foreign Affairs and Trade in 2013. They'd heard of FINCA, and I talked to them about my work with FINCA Uganda. I gave them a paper I'd written on microfinance and health insurance and I did a presentation, just on my laptop, to the two of them. After that, they started giving me work. In fact, they gave me more work than I could handle. As far as I could tell, I was the only microfinance specialist they'd come across who'd had experience running a microfinance bank. I guess it wasn't so much a matter of there being a lot of work; it was more that there weren't a lot of microfinance specialists around to do the work. It's a highly specialised sector. The leaders in the sector are people who say to you, 'So, what area do you specialise in? Micro-insurance? Payment services?' It's a real niche market.

Between staying on at FINCA for five more months and the consulting work, Jacqui and I spent much of 2002 apart. It wasn't good for either of us. Depending on short-term consultancies meant spending half the year overseas. I felt a bit of guilt about being away from the family so much, and it was tough, going it alone, travelling all the time. It was tough for Jacqui, too. Her parents, David and Joliette, moved to Australia soon after we first arrived in January. Her mum came first, and then her dad moved a little later after he'd sold their house. Having Jacqui's parents with us made a huge difference: without them, it would've been impossible for me to spend all that time travelling. But it was still hard for Jacqui. I'd phone home and hear her struggling to adjust to life in a new country with a three-year-old.

I guess I was also a bit lonely, working as an individual consultant. I think that's quite a common experience. I missed the collegiality of working in a team, and the sense of isolation was intensified by moving to Australia. When you migrate, one of the most important things you lose is your social capital, your networks: the people that matter to you, socially and professionally. The loss of social capital is one of your biggest costs – perhaps the biggest cost. Social capital takes time and effort to build up. I really felt that loss. Not just professionally, but also personally; I wanted to be part of the Australian community. I started looking around for an organisation – a home, if you like – in terms of my work. I began exploring what was out there.

∞

In those early months after moving to Sydney, Jacqui was particularly worried about finding a house suitable to settle in and bring up a family. She needed to make a nest, to have our own place and feel settled, so we spent July looking at houses. Houses were open for inspection on Wednesdays and Saturdays. We'd look through the newspaper on Sunday, Monday and Tuesday; we'd find houses that looked okay and circle them, and then we'd go and inspect them on Wednesday. On Wednesday night, Jacqui would cry. Then we'd look at the paper again on Thursday and Friday, and we'd go and inspect the houses on Saturday. On Saturday night, Jacqui would cry. But eventually we found the right house, the house that we're still in. Prices were going up rapidly, but this area – Belrose – was a little cheaper than Pymble, where we'd been renting. I was still a keen surfer and wanted to be near the beach. I liked this area, and it was a bit more affordable.

Shortly after we found the house, Jacqui fell pregnant. We moved into the house on my birthday, 6 September 2002, and that same evening, I had to leave for a six-week assignment in Africa. I left with the house in a complete shambles. It was very tough for Jacqui, who was about two months pregnant with our second child, but at least we had a home.

Our beautiful daughter, Brontë, was born on 23 March 2003. She was also premature, like Thomas; she was born six weeks early. I was away at the time, working in Indonesia. Jacqui has this line: 'Guy was in Bali and I was in labour!' I was working with the Central Bank of Indonesia on a GTZ-funded project, reviewing small banks known in Indonesia as BPRs – Bank Perkreditan Rakyat – literally meaning People's Credit Banks. The assignment was for about three weeks, and I was planning on getting back home a month before the birth. My job was to assess these BPRs. They're like community banks, somewhere between a cooperative bank and a commercial bank. There were too many of these BPRs registered in Bali, and the Central Bank wanted me to advise them which ones to close down.

So there I was in Bali, working on that project, when Jacqui phoned me one day to say, 'I think my waters have broken. I'm going to the hospital.' She phoned again the next day and said, 'False alarm! Nothing's happened.'

'Oh, okay,' I said. 'Well, just keep me posted.'

That was on a Thursday. I stayed in Indonesia, working on my assignment. And then around midnight on Saturday I got another phone call; Jacqui had gone into labour. I quickly cancelled the rest of that trip and rushed home.

I didn't make it back in time, unfortunately: Brontë was born early on Sunday morning and I didn't get there until Sunday night.

Brontë still brings it up, if we ever snap at each other: 'You weren't even there when I was born!'

We've got a picture of her in a shoe box – she was so tiny, as Thomas had also been. Both of them were worries at the beginning, but they have turned out just fine. More than fine!

Both the kids have great birthdays: Thomas's is nine, nine, nineteen ninety-nine, and Brontë's is twenty-three, three, two thousand and three!

∞

The non-profit sector beckoned again. I considered setting up a consultancy or an NGO on my own, but starting from scratch in Australia seemed impossible. I began putting out feelers with a few different organisations, like Opportunity International. I was given a verbal offer of a job with Opportunity, but on reflection I realised a couple of things. First, I'm not a practising Christian, so I didn't really want to join a faith-based organisation. Second, rather than joining another organisation, I realised I wanted to be in control. I'd been a leader in my previous two roles, with FINCA and Ntinga. I liked being the boss. I'd got used to it. It crossed my mind to apply for a CEO role at an NGO, but I couldn't find an NGO that was doing work in microfinance. In the meantime, FINCA offered me a position to run their program in China, but Jacqui was resolute: 'I'm not going anywhere!'

I started to pursue an idea that had been forming in my mind for a few months: establishing a World Education office in Australia. I began by following up my connections with World Education Incorporated in the US. Having visited their headquarters in Boston several times, I'd got to know a number of the staff. I was known by the senior managers from my work with World Education in South Africa – in particular on the Ntinga Program, for which I was the project director. My main contact in Boston was Gill Garb, a South African who'd been living in the States for thirty years. Gill had been out to South Africa a few times to work with me on the Ntinga Micro-Enterprise Program, and she put me in touch with David Kahler, the World Education vice president for Asia. David was very encouraging. He told me that World Education was interested in expanding their microfinance program in Asia, and geographically Australia was regarded as part of Asia. He recommended that I put together a proposal with a business plan and financial projections, and submit it to the World Education president, Joel Lamstein.

Over the next few months, David and I stayed in close touch, exploring different options. After many discussions, we agreed that World Education Australia would be set up as an NGO, a non-profit company limited by guarantee. By registering as an NGO in Australia, World Education Australia would potentially be eligible for funding under the Australian government's aid program. I prepared a detailed business plan outlining how the organisation would be formed, how it would operate, how it would be funded, and who would be on the board. My business plan was really an analysis of the risks and the benefits of establishing an independent affiliate of World Education Incorporated in Australia. The benefits for World Education were mainly around accessing new sources of funding from AusAID and the Australian public. As an offshoot of World Education Inc., I envisaged we'd be in a good position to match and leverage funding from other sources. The kind of strategy I envisaged was that I'd approach the US government and say, 'We've got this project in Nepal and we've got some funding from Australia. If you put in 75 per cent, we can put in 25 per cent.' And the US government would be more willing to fund us because sharing the cost would reduce their risk and give them leverage for future co-funding with Australia. Then I'd go along to AusAID and say, 'We've got this project in Nepal and the US government is funding 75 per cent of the cost. Can you put in the balance?'

In October 2002, I went back to Boston to discuss the proposal and to ask for a loan to fund the start-up. The main risk from World Education's point of view was that World Education Australia would go out on its own and cut its ties with the parent organisation, and they'd lose their investment. I had to persuade them that this wouldn't happen and that I'd make sure the relationship remained strong.

Joel Lamstein, the World Education president, wasn't a man to beat about the bush. 'Guy,' he said, 'your business plan's crap. Throw it out! But I believe in you. You did a great job for us in Africa. We'll handshake on the deal. Go do this thing!'

The proposal still needed the approval of the World Education board to go ahead. The board approved it a few weeks later on condition that I covered my salary, either through donations or through consulting work. They also agreed to give me a line of credit up to US$500,000. The microfinance adviser for World Education Africa resigned at around that time, so I then took over that role – as well as being the microfinance adviser for Asia.

∞

In February 2003, I travelled to south-east Asia and to South Africa, partly on a consultancy and partly to get to know the staff at World Education Asia. I started off in Cambodia, in Phnom Penh. David Kahler accompanied me on that trip. He had told me that Cambodia was fairly peaceful, and he was right; there wasn't a lot of violence, but there was a level of lawlessness that surprised me. There still is, but fourteen years ago was closer to the time of Vietnamese occupation, and there was still a sense of lawlessness. I remember the traffic was pretty crazy, as it still is – and the police didn't do much to control it. There weren't many traffic lights in Phnom Penh in those days, but where there were lights, no one paid them any attention. People drove straight through the reds. I didn't see anyone actually getting hurt, but I did see a car hitting a tuk-tuk – a three-wheeler motorcycle taxi. If you were speeding or went through a red light, and you were stopped by the police – which happened very rarely – you'd simply pay them. I saw that myself: a driver was stopped, and he just handed over a few riel, the local currency. Corruption was endemic; there's still a high level of corruption today. I remember reading in the paper about some buildings that had collapsed during construction. I don't think anyone was killed, but one or two construction workers were badly injured. There didn't seem to be much in the way of building regulations in place – or if there were, they weren't being followed. Some of the scaffolding used in building construction in Asia is made entirely of bamboo, tied together with rope. It's amazing how high they can make it: eight, nine, ten storeys! I know it's actually quite strong, but for the life of me I wouldn't like to go up it myself.

There were laws in place, of course, but law enforcement was lacking. World Education Asia paid taxes and social security benefits on behalf of their staff, but I heard there were a lot of businesses and individuals – including some expats – who weren't paying any taxes or social security benefits. It's been tightened up since then, but at that time paying taxes was almost optional.

The first morning that I was in Phnom Penh, I gave a presentation on microfinance to the staff at World Education Cambodia. I was surprised to discover that their knowledge of financial literacy was extremely limited: their ability to calculate interest rates, for example, or their understanding of the importance of savings, or how to budget. The basics of how business works: how you calculate profit, and how you calculate expenses. Basic financial literacy. There were language issues, of course, which exacerbated their difficulty in understanding what I was trying to explain. But the level of financial literacy was really low. It brought home to me early on just how important financial literacy is among the people we're working with.

∞

There's an old tradition in Cambodia, and in other parts of Asia, about using puppets to tell stories from ancient times; stories about battles and rulers and love lost. Mythological stories from ancient times. It's a tradition that's shared by many cultures, handing stories down through the generations, from parent to child.

I first became aware of this storytelling tradition in Cambodia on that trip in early 2003 when I attended a puppet show by a group known as the Cambodian Masters. The show was performed out in the open in a small public park. They'd set up a little theatre, with curtains across the stage, almost like the old Punch and Judy shows. The puppets were large, some quite grotesque, with exaggerated features; the 'baddies' were made to look hideous, and the 'goodies' beautiful. The performance was in Khmer, so I didn't understand a word. I was with a staff member from World Education Cambodia and I tried to get him to translate for me, but he was laughing so much during most of the performance that I missed a lot of what was being said. It didn't really matter, though. I thoroughly enjoyed the spectacle of the puppet show and the obvious delight of the rest of the audience.

When the Khmer Rouge were in power – that terrible time when twenty-five per cent of the population died from starvation and disease and murder – the traditional storytelling and the puppets virtually disappeared. A lot of the old puppet masters had been targeted for annihilation or re-education because the tradition represented the old ways, and the Khmer Rouge went to great lengths to eradicate the old and enforce the new. The puppet masters couldn't practice their skills at all during that period, so the tradition was almost completely lost. Then, when the Khmer Rouge were ousted in 1979 and peace was restored, a group of the puppet masters got together and formed a Cambodian Puppet Masters Association. They were generally men in their late fifties and sixties, committed to restoring the tradition of making puppets and telling the old stories through puppet shows.

I was so moved by what these older Cambodians were trying to do – bearing in mind the horrors they had lived through – that I started to support them myself with my own money. A colleague and I managed to find a couple of sponsors in Australia, as well as ourselves – but it didn't amount to a lot of money. A few thousand dollars, including our own. These old master puppeteers didn't need a lot of money. They were working on less than $300 a month.

This was fourteen years ago. Some of these old guys probably aren't still around. When they're gone, that'll be it. There'll be no one else to carry on the tradition. Watching one of those puppet shows, I felt like I was watching the last remnants of a dying culture. In a few years, it may disappear altogether. But there's a chance that this puppet tradition may survive. If I've been able to make any contribution to saving that tradition, I'm proud. The puppet masters were starting to teach younger people the art of puppet-making and performing. My colleague and I encouraged them to bring a more contemporary flavour to the storytelling so that the puppet shows would have wider appeal. We asked them to tell stories about important social issues like domestic violence, and how children who leave home at a young age to work in the town can be vulnerable to exploitation. Introducing stories that have relevance for a modern audience. A lot of kids wouldn't have ever seen puppet shows before; by making the stories more contemporary, we hoped to help bring an old cultural practice into the mainstream. It also enabled us to 'sell' the puppet shows to potential funders. Once audiences became more familiar with the performances, we were hoping that they'd be willing to pay a small entrance fee so that it would become a sustainable venture – a livelihood for the puppet masters. In fact, that's what has happened. There has been some success.

I had some interesting discussions with David Kahler on that trip about whether it's right for an outsider to come in and try to support local people to restore their own cultural traditions. Whether it's culturally sensitive, or culturally appropriate. Sometimes we'd talk late into the night. In the end, I guess what's important is simply to offer that support and see if it's wanted.

I saw some of the scripts later when we were trying to introduce new stories, or old stories with a new twist, to support educational purposes. That was a bit of a balancing act, trying to make these difficult topics as interesting as possible. We tried to get the puppet masters to perform a story with a message about practising safe sex, but they weren't happy with that. People were reluctant to talk about sex, so we gave up on that topic. One issue we focused on was the vulnerability of girls who leave the rural areas to go and work in garment factories or bars, where they're extremely vulnerable to exploitation and mistreatment. If they're told they won't get paid unless they agree to have sex with the customers, who are they going to turn to for help? Their parents aren't there and their villages are far away. We just wanted to try and point out the vulnerabilities of these girls when they don't have the support of their families and their communities. You can say things through a puppet which you couldn't say directly to someone, like getting a puppet to suggest where a young person – a school leaver, say – might start looking for a livelihood or business opportunity, when they've had no luck getting a job. The puppet might say, 'So, you've just finished school. That's great! You must be very proud. Now you need a job. You go to a shop and you ask the boss if they need anyone. And they say, do you have any experience? No? Okay, then we have no work for you. Then you go to another shop, and you get told the same thing. And after you've been looking all morning, you're hungry. You go and look for some rice. You can't find any. You look and look, and there's no rice to be found nearby. Now, there's a good business opportunity! You think to yourself, I can set up a little stall and sell rice and make some money!'

It makes me think of that story about this guy who was cleaning toilets. He'd been cleaning toilets in one of the big railway stations in London for many years. Then the council brought in a new rule: all their employees had to have a certain level of education and they had to be able to read and write. They went and checked all their employees, and when they came to the guy at the railway station, the guy who'd been cleaning toilets for years, they discovered he couldn't read and write. He could only sign his name. So they fired him. Very dejected, he got his things and began walking home, and then he thought, 'I really fancy a smoke. I haven't smoked for years, but I could do with one now.' So off he went to look for a pack of cigarettes, but he couldn't find a tobacconist. There wasn't one for miles. He said to himself, 'That's what I'll do with my retrenchment package: I'll set up a tobacconist.' And he did just that. He opened one near the railway station where he'd been cleaning toilets for years. It was a great success. He built it up, bought another one, and then another. After a few years, he was fairly wealthy. Then an opportunity came up to buy a whole chain of tobacconists. The man went to the bank to ask for a loan and the bank manager said, 'Sure, that's fine! Here's the loan agreement. Could you just read it through and then sign it?' And the man said, 'Actually, I can't read.' The bank manager said, 'What? You've got ten tobacconist shops and you're wealthy – and you can't read or write? Just imagine where you'd be if you knew how to read and write!' 'Yeah,' he said. 'I'd be cleaning toilets at the railway station.'

I like that story, but in fact not being able to read or write is an enormous hindrance to people's development. World Education Cambodia was working in another district, Kampong Chang, providing basic education and life skills to kids who had never been to school. Simple reading and writing. Over the last twenty or thirty years, there's been a huge upswing in literacy levels. In many countries in Asia, including Cambodia, literacy rates have improved enormously; Vietnam now has a literacy rate that's comparable with Australia's. But in some places, particularly in remote rural areas, there are still unacceptable numbers of people who can't read or write. Only about half of Nepalese women, for example, are functionally literate; that includes all those women living in urban areas who have been able to get an education. In the very remote rural areas, hardly any women can read or write. I remember thinking how providing literacy training would help them so much.

As an outsider, a foreigner, you interpret what you see in certain ways. And you're often wrong. I was travelling in Nepal once, with a Nepalese staff member from World Education Nepal. We travelled a fair way together, just the two of us, and we got to know each other quite well. From time to time, we passed groups of people waiting to catch a bus into the nearest town. I noticed there were many more men than women, and all the women were accompanied by a man – their husband, a brother, or maybe a son – and I interpreted this as evidence of women's oppression: the local culture didn't allow women to travel on their own.

I pointed this out to my Nepalese companion. Ramchandra Khanal was his name; a lovely old guy. He used to be the principal of a school before he worked as a field coordinator for World Education Nepal.

He responded, very politely, 'Yes, that might be the case…' He was very gentle with me, very diplomatic. He went on, 'It might be the case, but actually the reason is that the woman can't read or write. She can't read the bus timetable, and she can't read the number on the bus when it arrives. When she gets to the town, she can't read the street names or shop names.'

I thought to myself, why didn't I think of that? Of course, the fact that the women couldn't read or write reflected another form of oppression, but not in the obvious way that I had perceived it. It opened my eyes. It shows how wrong you can be, as a foreigner, making judgements or presumptions without knowing the full story. And I thought, you must listen more than you talk.

There was a woman that I met in a remote village in rural Nepal on that same trip. She was in her early twenties and she had a baby. Her husband was working as a waiter in Kathmandu and he was sending money back to her in the village. He would write to her and she would get someone to read the letter. On this occasion, Ramchandra read the letter to her.

In his gentle, respectful way, he later told me, 'The letter was quite formal and stilted because the husband knew someone else will be reading it.'

I don't know whether it would be usual for a husband in rural Nepal to write 'I love you' in a letter, but the letters from this woman's husband contained nothing personal because he didn't want other people in the village to know their business.

On our invitation, this young woman started attending literacy training run by World Education. A few months later, she told me she could read her husband's letters herself, and she could write back to him. My heart warmed at that, knowing we had made a difference to her life. She could tell him of her worries and her fears, and that she loved him. And he could write back and tell her that he was coming home soon and he'd bring back this and that and they would start their own business. It's so fundamental, being able to read and write. They're essential skills for business, whatever that story about the toilet cleaner-cum-tobacconist says. The truth is that people who can't read and write are very seldom successful in business.

Literacy is a necessary skill, but it's not sufficient to run a small business. That's where training in livelihood development and microfinance come in. We've often made the assumption in the past that people who come and do our training in microfinance and livelihoods can read and write, but that's not always the case. They often have very limited literacy skills, so we've modified much of our training to make it accessible to those people, using pictures, cartoons…and now we're using iPads and chatbots, that kind of thing. A lot of the work we've done in Nepal has been anchored in literacy training, followed up by livelihood training and microfinance.

I'm constantly reminded from my work – first in Africa and then in Asia – how important literacy is as a foundation skill, and how many women are still illiterate today, especially those living in rural areas. The fact is that a lot more men can read and write because more investment is made in educating male children than female children.

From my point of view, that isn't acceptable. When we work in rural communities, we try to persuade the families to send their girl children to school. But when we do that, we're making a judgement about the local culture and local values. We make judgements about domestic violence; we make judgements about following the law; we make judgements about empowerment.

After all these years of working in development, in poor communities in Asia and Africa, my conclusion is that some of these judgements are not correct. For example, the view that patriarchal systems or an imbalance in power relations are bad: they might not be such a good thing, but you can't assume you understand the values of another culture. What right do you have, coming in and challenging the local culture or rejecting certain values, based on the limited understanding you have as a foreign visitor? Who are you to judge? Of course, there are some absolutes for me: domestic violence, or not allowing your girl children to go to school. These things are completely unacceptable to me. But as a foreigner working in another culture, I accept that I bring my own values to bear on a situation. We all do. It's unavoidable. But I also think we have a responsibility to question those values and judgements. We need to ask ourselves whether it's right to impose those values on others.

# 7

# The nuts and bolts of microfinance

'Microfinance is an idea whose time has come' – Kofi Annan

I'm in Sydney on family business and arrange to meet with Guy on Saturday morning at his home in Belrose. The focus this morning is on the nuts and bolts of microfinance: how it works, why it works, and why it's so fundamental to changing the lives of the poor.

But today he's not in good shape. The sparkle has gone out of him. When he greets me at the front gate, I can see a change in him. The drugs have bloated his face and neck; a rash is visible on his wrists and the backs of his hands. He looks washed-out, exhausted. He confesses it's been a bad week: the rash is driving him crazy. Despite the antihistamines he takes morning and night, it's spread all over his body and it's madly itchy. He scratches until he bleeds. At its worst, it prevents him from sleeping. Sometimes, he says, the itch is worse than the pain. This is an unavoidable side effect from the drugs. But the drugs are keeping him alive.

He's also had what he calls 'kidney problems'. He says he had it investigated earlier in the week and was told to drink more water. Raising his cup, he tells me he's trying to drink more fluids – in all forms.

I suggest we postpone our conversation, but Guy insists we push on. He leads the way into the living room adjoining the kitchen, overlooking the back deck and the garden. Dark leather sofas form an L–shape around a large glass coffee table. On this cold June morning, the room is chilly.

Guy walks over to the far corner of the living room, where a small gas heater stands next to the sliding glass doors to the garden. He fiddles with the controls. 'Sorry, Sally – it's a bit cold in here, isn't it? It should heat up soon...'

He offers me tea and goes back to the kitchen to fill the kettle and get out mugs and teabags. He paces restlessly, hovering between kettle and fridge.

We chat about this and that. A few minutes later, mugs in hand, we return to the living room and the leather sofas. We're followed closely by two of the small canine family members, April and Chloe – one eager to be friends, the other holding back, watchful and anxious. The moment I sit, April leaps up beside me, all tail-wagging and happy panting. I stroke her soft, reddish fur and she snuggles closer.

Guy shoos her off quickly – 'Don't let her up. She won't leave you alone!' – and then winces slightly as he pulls a chair closer to where I'm sitting. Wincing is not Guy's thing.

I ask if he's in pain.

'No...well, not really. Just this tumour in my back...'

I wrap cold hands around my mug.

Guy twists an arm to reach behind his back, just below the shoulder blade on his left side. 'You can feel it. Here... Are you squeamish?' He turns away and pulls up his sweater and shirt.

Just below the left shoulder blade, the skin is stretched over a flattish oval lump about five centimetres long, three wide.

I apologise for cold fingers and touch the skin tentatively. The lump is smooth, hard. It feels deceptively harmless, like a slightly bulging muscle. The idea of it is sinister, but the slight protuberance appears innocent enough.

'Has it grown quickly?'

'Yeah, quite quickly. It seems to have stabilised now, though. My oncologist decided not to operate. We'll just monitor it... I had tumours there before, and they broke a couple of ribs. That was painful. I hoped they wouldn't come back.'

Then, in typical Guy style, he shrugs and pulls his shirt and jumper down briskly. The subject is closed.

∞

The idea in microfinance is that the services you offer should be as accessible as possible. You need to remember you're working with the poor and for the poor, so you want the services to be affordable by people on very low incomes. At the same time, though, you've got to charge enough to cover your costs so you can continue to offer the services, year after year. That means your interest rates and your fees need to be high enough to be financially secure and keep the services running. You can't rely on external funders, like other development projects. If you rely on external money, ultimately it's going to run out and the services will fall apart.

There's institutional sustainability as well. Your staff need to have the education, skills and experience to do the job, and you need systems and regulations and so on. But you've also got to keep your costs low enough to be affordable. That's the question: what is affordable? Keeping the services affordable means being as efficient as possible. Efficiency means keeping costs low while still giving a good service.

The costs for any financial institution are really threefold. One is the cost of doing business: the transaction costs. The cost of processing a $35 loan is much higher per unit dollar than the cost of doing a loan of $100,000: much, much higher. Take the example of getting a home loan from a major Australian bank: I know from my own experience in the past that they charge a mobilisation admin fee; in my case, it was $600. That's to cover the cost of risk assessment and paperwork and so on. On a home loan, a $600 admin fee is fair enough, but if you did a complex risk assessment for a $35 loan, that'd be crazy – it'd be ridiculous! The unit cost per dollar lent would be really high. The reason the unit cost is so high is because the operational costs of running a business are very high – the salary costs, the overheads, and everything else. So the unit cost for small loans is really high.

The second cost that's faced by any financial institution is the cost of loans not being repaid. One of the ways that financial institutions make money, of course, is to take money in. We used to have this saying about bankers: you borrow money from the public, you pay interest at three per cent, you lend at six per cent, and you go and play golf at three o'clock! In other words, you make money on the margin.

One of the ways that banks get repaid is by having collateral. That's why they ask you questions about your assets.

Remember Audrey, the woman who had her money eaten by rats? She had a loan, but she had no collateral. She was making around $2 a day; maybe $700 or $800 a year. With her husband's income, the family was making maybe $1,500 a year – in other words, they were just making ends meet. It's really tough. Not only did Audrey not have any collateral, she didn't have the means to do the paperwork that the banks require. The banks themselves would just say they couldn't take the risk.

That's the problem: the banks can't lend the money if there's a high risk of not being repaid, because if they don't get repaid the whole system would collapse. Not only do they need to get loans repaid, they also need the net interest on the loan – that three per cent – to cover their costs. And that's assuming they're getting one hundred per cent of the loan back. If they don't get the principle back, that's an even bigger problem.

The third cost facing all financial institutions is the cost of capital: the money you have to pay in order to borrow the money that you're lending out. Where does that money come from? In microfinance institutions, it generally comes from two sources. One source is the owner's equity capital. For an organisation like FINCA, a lot of that capital comes from donors, but also it comes from retained earnings – essentially your net assets. That's assets minus liabilities. The second source of capital is from your savings, a much bigger source of capital. The capital is invested – thereby earning interest – through loans to their customers. The problem, of course, is that with microfinance programs, your customers are poor people on very low incomes, and poor people don't save as much as they borrow. When you're running a big institution with tens of thousands of clients, some people have more savings and less loans, while other people have more loans and less savings, and you intermediate to manage that flow. In village banking, the groups cover a lot of the cost of the risk, and they help to reduce the transaction costs, but they don't really cover the cost of capital. The cost of mobilising savings is really high. You might still pay five per cent on savings, as you would at a bank. But instead of the individual members having to go to a bank, the loans officer goes out to the group, which means those people don't need to travel long distances to go into town to do their banking.

Organising people into groups helps to cover these costs. If you've got a group of thirty people, each borrowing $100, instead of processing thirty loans of $100, you're doing one single $3,000 loan, which of course reduces the unit cost.

Now, with the second cost, the risk of not being repaid, what a lot of banks do is get to know you. They want to know how much you earn and they ask you a lot of questions about your assets. They want verification – pay slips, property valuations, that sort of thing. That all costs money. A lot of the costs associated with a loan application are related to getting to know you. In microfinance, or village banking, the person who's going to know you best in your village is usually your neighbour, who has been living alongside you in the village for the last thirty years. Who knows you better than your neighbour? That is the basis for peer collateral. Within the group, if one person doesn't pay, the other people in the group pay for you. The risk is borne by the group as a whole, not piecemeal. So if there are three people who can't repay their $100, other people pay for them, and they then make a deal between them for the loan to be repaid.

For example, Audrey told me she sells a lot more cloth at one time of the year than another, and the other people in her group know her business works like that. She borrows money from the group to tide her over when her business is slow and things are tight. She pays the loan back later, when sales pick up. And the other members of the group do the same at different times, depending on their kind of business and when cash flow is slow, or when it's picked up. That means the loans follow different cycles.

One of the problems with the group approach is that everyone is on the same loan term, maybe a one-year loan term. But your production cycle, or your business cycle, might not be geared to a one-year loan term. If you're a rice farmer, for example, you might get one harvest a year; but if you're a material buyer and seller, you might go through your working capital four times a year. So, depending on your production or business cycle, you actually could have a larger loan over the year, or you could have a shorter period to pay it back. In other words, the group approach means the loan isn't tailored for you in particular: it's not client-focused, if you like. But apart from that, the group approach works very well – particularly around peer collateral. Repayment rates are excellent: in most good practice microfinance programs, they're above ninety-five per cent.

But there's a downside to peer collateral as well. In Australia, if I take out a loan with a bank and fail to repay, I may end up being declared a bankrupt. It doesn't look good. But what do I really care? There are no major consequences for me, and after a few years everything goes back to normal. But for Audrey, and other women like her in village banks, if she doesn't repay her loan, her family and friends would get involved. Members of her group have covered her loan in anticipation that she'll pay them back. She'd be letting them down. She'd be criticised by her family and friends and possibly ostracised in her community. The consequences could be terrible. That's what peer collateral is: it's family, it's friends, and it's your neighbour. The pressure exerted by peer collateral can be so intense that it's led to deep rifts in families and communities. It's even led to suicides. The dynamics of the group reflect the dynamics of the village. If the village dynamics aren't good, then the group dynamics aren't good. If the group isn't going well, the effects can spill over into other relationships within that village, and vice versa.

Group dynamics are often fluid and changeable. The loans officers with FINCA needed to understand these dynamics and help the savings group to manage them. Sometimes when members didn't get along, groups would break up or dissolve completely, and the people who didn't get along would join different groups. The groups that grew and stayed strong were generally those that were stable, where the members had known each other well for a long time. Although there were instances where relationships within a savings group and within a village were difficult and volatile, or where conflict festered, people generally seemed to get along. That's true in most communities. It's not just because people are inherently good; it's because there's a fundamental need for them to get along. The dynamics of a savings group or a community are driven by the fact that people depend on each other.

∞

In village banking, it's important to start with savings. The group dynamic develops with savings: the members start by saving together, just small amounts – maybe 20 or 30 cents per week. You collect their savings each week, and the group learns to trust you and to trust each other. Then, after a while, the members say to themselves and each other, 'Do we really trust this FINCA group? Let's get all our savings back and see if they've really got it.' They test you and they test each other. Their savings accumulate for the next three months. Then, after they've saved enough and have built up a good reserve, a few of the members take out a small loan; that gets repaid over time, and then they take out a bigger loan, and then an even bigger loan.

When members start borrowing around $800 or $1,000 each, two things can happen: one is that it starts becoming cost-effective to graduate them into an individual loan program, more like a conventional bank loan. An individual loan can of course be more tailor-made to meet their specific needs. The second thing that can happen is that there are increasing differences between the members in terms of what they can borrow, or what they want to borrow. One person might have a $1,000 loan, while the rest of the group together might have savings of around $4,000 in total. This means that the person borrowing $1,000 isn't realistically carrying a guarantee by the rest of the group. If the borrower defaulted, the others might not be able to cover the loan – and they almost certainly wouldn't want to cover the loan. So, when someone wants to start borrowing larger amounts, you need to help them graduate up to the next level – like enabling them to take out a loan from a commercial bank.

Sometimes, people take out loans they can't afford. Like people everywhere, they overstretch themselves and then have problems repaying. Taking out a big loan can be a way of saying to the other members in their group, 'My business is doing so well, I can afford a bigger loan than you!' The dynamics are the same, wherever you are, whether it's a small town in rural England or a village in a remote part of Uganda. Pride, jealousies, petty squabbles – the dynamics are the same. To me, people are much the same everywhere; there are more similarities than differences. The differences are cultural overlays. In many parts of Africa, looking someone in the eye is considered aggressive. But in modern Australia, avoiding eye contact is unfriendly and makes people uncomfortable. In southern Africa and East Africa, if you want to go past people who are talking to each other, you walk between them – because you shouldn't go behind someone's back. In other cultures, like our own, walking between people in conversation would be considered rude. There are many, many small nuances of difference between cultures and subcultures. Ultimately it's about learning to live and work together.

The group village banking methodology was developed by FINCA. There are many other methodologies, like the solidarity lending methodology, used by the Grameen Bank, which involves smaller groups – typically, six groups of five members each, operating separately and together as a larger group of thirty people. Other methodologies involve smaller groups, larger groups, subgroups, three-people groups, six-people groups – many different variations. Each approach has its strengths and weaknesses.

Successful microfinance programs work by covering their own

costs, and the thing about covering your costs is that there are strong economies of scale – not only within one group, but by creating many groups. As a result, many microfinance institutions have pushed to create more groups, and they've also tried to push those groups to take out more loans. That has led to some bad outcomes. In Uttar Pradesh, in Central India, over-indebtedness led to a number of suicides. That's how bad it was, because with savings and loans groups, the pressure isn't from a bank, it's from your family and your community. That's the nature of solidarity lending: your neighbour is relying on you to repay your loan so that they'll be able to get loans in future. If you don't pay, they'll go to your mother or another family member to complain that you're not making your repayments. The pressure can be unrelenting. People can be put under huge stress, leading to arguments and fights between group members and sometimes the breakdown of the group.

Banking is a complicated business. Village banking – banking on a small scale – is complicated too. It takes years of experience and technical training to understand the way group methodologies work, how risk needs to be managed, and how to run a program as efficiently as possible. I've seen large not-for-profit organisations get into microfinance and fail. I've seen smaller charitable organisations, faith-based and other organisations, who try and give microfinance a go: they want to do good and they see the value of microfinance. Because they managed many projects in the past – large and small, simple and complex – they assumed they could also manage microfinance projects. But they often fail too, because they don't understand even the basics of what I've been talking about.

Some microfinance agencies charge really high fees, and they do it because they're inefficient. They are run badly and they pass their inefficiencies on to their clients. Their justification is that costs are much higher than revenue. That's when microfinance agencies have really stood on the backs of poor people in order to cover their costs.

But in spite of these challenges, microfinance services genuinely have the potential to change people's lives for the better. Unlike many other development interventions, successful microfinance programs are sustainable in the longer term, after external support has been withdrawn. And, as I always say, if it's worth helping one person – one Audrey – then it's worth helping tens of thousands or hundreds of thousands of people. In other words, to make a substantial difference you need to go to scale. I call it 'horizontal outreach'. Of course, going to scale makes it more complicated.

At FINCA Uganda, we were supporting about twelve hundred savings groups of about thirty women each, on average. That's about forty thousand women altogether. We kept a record of the savings and loans of every one of those women. Some of the woman, say in the southern part of the country, were engaging in vegetable gardening and had rapid turnover, while other women in the north were involved in longer-term agricultural projects, maybe rice farming or coffee growing. We then had to manage the fund flows between these different production cycles, to make sure that we'd always have cash available when someone needed to draw down on their savings. It's a technical business; banking is a highly technical business.

For me, working in a development bank for a few years was wonderful experience. I learned an enormous amount. I made mistakes, of course, but at least they weren't serious. I might've made serious mistakes if my colleagues and boss had allowed that to happen! I learned from their experience, fortunately, rather than at the cost of poor people.

∞

Historically, microfinance has focused on women. There are practical reasons for that. I don't think that women are inherently better repayers than men. A more practical reason is that women are less migratory than men. Because of children, family responsibilities, group dynamics, traditional practices – a whole range of social and cultural reasons – women don't up and leave. Men, on the other hand, tend to come and go; they move to the city or to other parts of the country to get work, leaving their wives and children behind.

The second reason for focusing on women is that they are better development recipients. Women look after the children, they look after their families, their homes – and they look after the men! Experience shows that if you focus on women, you get much better outcomes in health, education, nutrition, shelter. Infant mortality is reduced if you focus your development intervention on women. These results are borne out by empirical research. I think that's a much better reason to focus on women than simply because they're better repayers.

There's a third reason why women historically have been the focus of microfinance programs. If your objective is to reduce poverty, then women should be your focus, because women are poorer than men. Rural women are poorer than urban women, so if you have a pro-poor mission, then you're more likely to focus on rural women.

Microfinance doesn't just make women less poor. Microfinance gives women more power. I'm not an anthropologist or a sociologist, but it's been pretty clear to me that poor women are disempowered. In a lot of the poor rural areas I've worked in, women won't talk in a public meeting unless they're directly spoken to; they wait until all the men have finished talking before they make a comment. They look at the ground and won't look you in the eye. And that's just the tip of the iceberg. There's a huge amount of research on how women – poor rural women especially – are disempowered.

Microfinance programs change gender dynamics. Belonging to a savings group gives women confidence. The women know that the loans officer, who may be a man, depends on them for his livelihood, and that if they don't repay a loan or they don't work together as a group, he may lose his job. Taking on a leadership role in the group as the chairman, secretary or treasurer gives women skills, and it gives them status. Having access to loans and savings helps women grow their businesses and make more money.

From observation, and from what I've read, it's clear that

microfinance programs often have a huge impact on women's individual lives. Surprisingly often, women who stand for office on their local village or town council have a history of belonging to a microfinance program. That's where they learned to operate in a group; that's where they gained confidence. There's evidence that being an active member of a microfinance program helps women to feel more empowered. We've done studies on the impacts of microfinance programs on communities and individuals, and we have found that women who are members of a savings and loans group are more likely to occupy leadership roles in their communities than women who are not members.

I believe that microfinance is more empowering than other forms of aid. Microfinance creates an adult–adult relationship. You have to treat people as customers, not simply as aid recipients. Of course, the way you deliver aid, the methods and processes you use, makes a huge difference; the way you engage with people, for example; the way you conduct needs assessments. You can't empower people if you follow disempowering processes, or processes that don't engage with people as equals. A process where you have to treat your clients or customers as equals, and not just as passive recipients of aid, is going to achieve a better outcome all round.

∞

A lot of aid projects are time-dependent: there's a start date and an end date. You do what you can in that time frame and then move on. Everyone knows that the project is going to end. But microfinance is forever. The loans officer might change, and the group membership might change; but the microfinance institution will be there for many years – perhaps a whole lifetime. It's not just a project; it's a long-term relationship. That completely changes the dynamics.

Education and health services are critical. But the truth is that there simply isn't enough funding to ensure that everyone gets access to quality health, education and other services. In development work, you've got to make choices: choices about what you do, where you work, how much you can achieve. You choose to provide maternity services in one village, or anti-malaria drugs in another village. Those choices mean that other villages will miss out. Your choices are life-and-death choices for those villages. In one village, women will give birth with trained birth attendants, and little kids will be treated for malaria. In another village, mothers will continue to die in childbirth and malaria will still claim lives. I don't want to be faced with those choices. That's part of what attracted me to microfinance.

The wonderful thing about microfinance is that you can build it to scale. Unlike education and health and other essential services, the cost of providing microfinance services can be covered by the end user – the beneficiaries, in many cases people on very low incomes. You lend someone $500 and you charge them twenty per cent interest, so they pay back $600 over a year. That additional $100 covers your costs, so you can lend to more people. Instead of helping one or two people, or a hundred, or even a thousand, you can help literally millions of people today. There are two billion adults of working age in the world today who have no access to banking services. Microfinance services have the potential to change all that. Microfinance can literally change the world, make life better for millions – even billions – of people.

The other thing about microfinance is that it's sustainable over time. If people can repay loans and cover the costs of savings services, insurance and payment services, then you can provide those service not only today, or this year, but next year and the year after and the year after that. That's vertical provision, if you like. That's not necessarily true of other services. I don't want to understate the importance of education and health services; they're obviously essential for any community. I just want to highlight one of the differences between financial services and other ways of helping to alleviate poverty.

The question then comes down to how much poor people can afford to pay and how much they should pay. That's the art of microfinance:

finding the balance between charging enough interest to cover your costs and keeping it low enough to make it affordable.

This will surprise a lot of people, but empirical research indicates that the returns from very small businesses, like growing vegetables or fishing or running little market stalls, are in the range of two hundred to seven hundred per cent a year! Take the example of a woman who buys and sells vegetables at the local market. One day she buys $10 worth of vegetables and sells them for $12, so she's made twenty per cent profit on her vegetables. The next day she buys $12 worth of vegetables, and again she makes twenty per cent profit on the sale of her vegetables. The next day she makes another twenty per cent profit, and so on, every day, for two hundred days of the year. Compounded over a year, that's four thousand per cent! The point is that woman may be on a low income, and she may be uneducated – but she's not stupid. She knows that if she's making four thousand per cent profit on her vegetables, she can borrow at thirty, forty or even fifty per cent a year and still make a profit. What's important is that she has access to loans when she needs the money. In fact, as long as she can keep selling her vegetables, and she's making a return of say two hundred per cent a year, then logically she should borrow as much as she can – even at interest rates as high as forty or fifty per cent a year.

Debt can be a burden, of course. Over-indebtedness can be a real problem, whether you're rich or poor. But reducing the burden of debt for poor people isn't just about keeping interest rates low. It's also about consumer protection – making the debt as least risky as possible – and about good money management. The first thing to understand is that you should only borrow for emergencies and for investments. If you're using debt for consumption, then all you're doing is digging a big hole for yourself. That's true whether you're a wealthy person in Sydney or a poor farmer in Bangladesh. Imagine that woman selling vegetables in the market has a young daughter, and that daughter gets malaria. Medical services aren't free in many of the countries we work in. The woman needs to take her daughter to hospital, and she'll need to pay for medicines. This is where access to borrowings is so vital – much more important than the interest rate she'll be charged on her loan. To get medical treatment for her daughter, the woman will gladly pay interest of forty, fifty or sixty per cent, or even much more. Say she borrows $10, and at the end of the following week she's required to repay that amount plus interest of another $10. She'll do it gladly, if she's able, to save her daughter's life – although the annualised interest rate amounts to ten thousand per cent!

Although I agree that we need to keep interest rates low, access to loans and consumer protection are just as important. Loans need to be accessible in a way that protects the vulnerable person. That means giving people knowledge. It's also about the rules and regulations imposed by the central government. Of course, some of the consumer protection legislation that we take for granted in Australia isn't offered in other countries, unfortunately. This is why savings services are really important; in fact, more important than loans.

∞

One thing you'll notice, if you spend time in a rural area of any developing country, is that people are often involved in many different enterprises. They do a bit of rice farming; they do a bit of vegetable farming. They raise chickens and pigs, or a goat or two, or a buffalo. They sell the eggs and the chickens and milk. They run a small store. They might also do some casual work as an unskilled labourer in the nearest town. They don't specialise in any one thing. People are rational, so they reduce their risk of one business failing, and it helps them to manage their cash flow so they earn a little bit of income over time.

Not having access to savings services is one of the main factors that keeps people poor. If they get access to savings, all other things being equal, they should be better off because they are able to focus on fewer, more profitable enterprises or work more productively.

Access to savings and loans is not simply about where you live.

It's also about the social and cultural and economic factors that affect people's lives.

Take the example of a woman living in a remote part of rural Cambodia. She's had very little education. She can't read or write. She's hardly travelled outside her village. Imagine how impossibly difficult it would be for her to approach a conventional bank. She may not even know what services a bank could provide. She might not understand the full value of savings and believes herself to be too poor to be able to save. The idea of borrowing money would seem impossible – completely beyond her reach.

Improving people's access to financial services is something I've worked hard on: not only in terms of the service provision itself, but also in terms of the emotional and psychological aspects. Access in that sense has a lot to do with people's knowledge: their financial education, their financial capability, their ability to calculate what the bank is going give them, how much interest rates cost and how much a loan will really cost them. I want to help poor people access financial services, not only by providing those services in ways that would work for them, but also through education – by which I mean technical and vocational skills, skills around running a small business better, understanding budgeting and marketing and costing, knowing when you're making a profit.

It always surprised me how some poor people, once we provided them with some early basic training, would scratch their heads and work out that they were actually making a loss in one business, and they'd be better off closing that business down. The reason they wouldn't know that they'd been making a loss was because the money they and their husband or wife were earning from different activities – from farming, from casual labouring, or from working as a waiter or a maid or some other casual job – that money was all going into the same pot. They didn't realise that some of their income streams – the chicken business or the vegetable business or the casual labouring – were more profitable than others, and one or more of those income streams was making a loss. They also didn't realise, of course, which of their income streams were making more money. Once they had the right skills and they were able to access savings and loans, they could focus more on their more profitable activities.

My take on development is this: a lot of the decisions being made in the development sector – decisions around what kinds of intervention to provide, who to provide it to, and where – are made by professionals and bureaucrats. Those decisions are not being made by the beneficiaries themselves – the poor people we are trying to help. Ultimately, my measure of good development is when people make decisions about their own lives, when they have both the income and the ability to make decisions about their lives and their children's lives. Success is when people don't need to rely on external support. They can rely on their own wherewithal, their own skills and access to sustainable services. That makes for a more equitable relationship between donor and beneficiary. That's always been an important aspect of microfinance for me.

In 2007 I published a book on microfinance, *Conversations with Practitioners: The challenges of market-led microfinance*, which was commissioned by MicroSave, an international financial inclusion consulting firm which operates across Asia and Africa. It was based on interviews I conducted with microfinance leaders and practitioners in Africa and Asia, focusing on how and why microfinance institutions should be market-led, responding to the needs of clients. Whenever I have talked about writing another book, Jacqui reminds me that when I was writing *Conversations with Practitioners*, I asked her to shoot me if I ever suggested doing another one! I much prefer doing the work rather than writing about it. But I'm proud of that book. It reflects my own philosophy on microfinance: it's about seeing poor people as clients whose views count just as much as anyone else's. And it's about seeing our role as serving our clients and trying to meet their needs.

∞

When I was managing director of FINCA Uganda, the chief operations officer who was responsible for the loans and savings programs came into my office and told me a story I've never forgotten.

At that time, we were supporting around twelve hundred savings groups, each consisting of thirty to thirty-five members. That's a significant number of people: around forty thousand clients. Most of these groups met regularly – every week, or every fortnight, sometimes once a month. The word got around that we'd helped to establish these groups, and a few development agencies involved in health and education programs approached us. They wanted access to these groups because they provided an efficient way of reaching a large number of people. Working with these groups meant they could save themselves the cost of mobilising communities themselves. One of these agencies, a large international development agency, arranged to deliver antenatal education and training to one of our groups. The vast majority of the group members in that particular program were women, so antenatal education was an important development priority. The loans officer responsible for managing that group told the members about the antenatal training and asked them whether they were interested. The women all confirmed they were keen to receive the training. Our staff then arranged with the development agency when and where they should deliver the training.

On the appointed day, our loans officer arrived at the village a few minutes before eight o'clock. She facilitated the meeting, which finished as scheduled at a quarter to nine. At ten to nine, there was no sign of anyone from the international development agency. Nine o'clock, and the trainer still hadn't arrived. A quarter past nine, still no one. The women were all waiting with the loans officer in the hot sun. Some of them had babies and toddlers with them; the kids were getting restless. The women had work they needed to be getting back to: meals to prepare, crops to tend, small businesses to run. The minutes ticked by and some members of the group started to drift away. Twenty-five past nine, and the trainer finally arrived.

Our loans officer said to the trainer, 'What happened? We've been waiting here for twenty-five minutes!'

And the trainer said, 'What's your problem? You're not paying for this!'

Of course, that was the attitude of that particular individual. I'm not saying the agency shared the same attitude. But the point is that in microfinance, the loans officers who are working with the clients know that it's the clients who are covering the costs of the service through the interest they pay on their loans. The loans officers know they need to provide a good service to the clients, and the clients know that because they're paying for the service – including the salary of the loans officer – they can expect to receive a good service. More and more organisations are offering microfinance services these days, so if the clients are dissatisfied they can move to another provider. People are not just recipients of development; they are active players in that development.

What it boils down to is the power relationship between the financial services provider and the client, or the beneficiary. Ultimately, my aim is to change that power relationship. I want to change the lives of poor people. If they have more money, they're better off. And if they're better off, they can make decisions about their own lives. And to make the right decisions – right for them and their families and their communities – they need knowledge and they need support. That's real empowerment.

# 8

# Making it happen

'Money won't create success, the freedom to
make it will' – Nelson Mandela

Back in Sydney, working from my little study upstairs at home, I spent the second half of 2003 setting up World Education Australia, working through all the legal requirements. In the meantime, I continued working as a consultant, travelling much of the time.

I registered World Education Australia as a public company limited by guarantee on 13 September 2003. From then until June 2004, when our first audit took place, I made $154,000 in consulting fees. Out of that, my salary was $90,000. I used the remainder to employ an administrator and to pay legal fees to get the organisation going.

Around the same time, AusAID engaged me to lead a team to review a microfinance project in Qinghai province in western China. The project was funded by the Australian government, through the aid program, and was being run by the Agricultural Bank of China. The team doing the evaluation was made up of Sun Ruomei, a microfinance specialist and researcher at the Chinese Academy of Social Sciences; a monitoring and evaluation specialist; an interpreter, and myself. We were accompanied on the mission by the project manager, Shane Nichols, an AusAID staff member at the Australian Embassy in Beijing. Shane was responsible for managing AusAID's program in Mongolia.

I arrived late to our first meeting at the Australian embassy, in a bit of a fluster. I'd mislaid my passport somewhere. It might've been stolen out of my jacket pocket, or maybe I just dropped it somewhere. The team was due to travel to Qinghai in a couple of days, and all foreigners are required to have a passport in order to fly within China.

I was still using my South African passport at that time, so I had to spend the next two days at the South African embassy, waiting for them to issue me with a temporary passport. I had to get a new visa as well. It was a hell of a business. Shane, the AusAID project manager, was incredibly calm and patient about the whole thing. As soon as I was issued with a temporary passport, I travelled with Shane and the other members of the team to Qinghai, starting with a visit to the microfinance institution working on the project.

Shane remembers how Guy immediately put them at their ease. 'Being evaluated by a foreign government agency was bound to have caused the staff at the microfinance institution to feel anxious. I remember him being very jovial and joking around, telling a few gags. And then he gave a presentation to explain how the evaluation would be conducted. He connected his laptop with the projector, and the first thing that popped up on the screen was a baby photo! Then he started talking about his kids and everybody got to see Thomas and Brontë, and that immediately lifted the whole mood.'

Shane told me later that my ability to put people at ease and be equally open and friendly with whoever I meet was one of his strongest first impressions of me. We travelled from village to village over the next two weeks, meeting village chiefs and interacting with the villagers – in particular the women who belonged to the savings groups. This is the part of my work that I enjoy most: taking the time to sit and talk with local people, learn about their lives, and share stories and experiences. Many of the local villagers spoke the local dialect and couldn't speak Mandarin, so we needed a local interpreter to translate from the local dialect into Mandarin, and then from Mandarin into English.

Sun Ruomei and I sat down with the local loans officer, who did the translating, and a small group of women from the village. We asked them about their businesses and livelihoods, and what their hopes and aspirations were. We also tried to find out how much interaction they had with the microfinance program. I remember asking one of the villagers a question about whether their business had grown in the last three years in terms of its turnover. I asked the question through Sun Ruomei, so that she could then ask the question in Mandarin to the loans officer. She and the loans officer then had a five-minute conversation in Mandarin. The loans officer turned to the villager and they spoke in the local dialect for another five minutes. Then the loans officer turned back to Sun Ruomei and spoke in Mandarin for two or three minutes. Finally, Sun Ruomei turned to me and said, 'Yes'!

At the end of the mission, I gave a presentation at the Australian embassy to AusAID staff and to various Chinese officials, including senior staff from the Agricultural Bank. I remember asking about the bank's capital adequacy ratio – the CAR, as it's known in the banking industry.

The CAR is about the relationship between a bank's equity and the amount it's lending. It's an important risk measure: if you don't have much equity, but you have a lot of loans, if some of those loans start going bad then there's a greater risk that you'll make losses, and you may even need to use people's savings to keep the bank operating. If the CAR is low, that means there's more risk, but it also means you are getting greater leverage, and most likely bigger returns, so you could charge lower interest rates. If the CAR is high, that means there's less risk, but it also means there are lower returns, so you generally need to charge higher interest on your loans, all other things being equal. These are the kinds of relationships and issues around how banks operate that I've noticed development agencies often don't understand.

Anyway, I was asking about the CAR, and the interpreter couldn't understand what I was talking about. I tried to explain what the CAR is. The interpreter did her best, but she had a real struggle trying to translate the technical terms. Then the officials started to ask questions. That was when things got really complicated. The interpreter turned to me for help, but of course I didn't know what the officials were asking. It was all getting rather frustrating.

Then Shane, the AusAID project manager, stepped in and said, 'Could I just make a comment?' He not only knew how to speak Chinese fluently, he also understood all the technical terms and was able to explain them in Chinese.

I thought, wow! This guy is good! I was really impressed. His manner also impressed me: his calmness and composure, his general air of quiet confidence. Being an AusAID staff member working for the Australian government, he was supposed to remain independent; his role on the evaluation was just to provide oversight and logistical support. But he came to our rescue in that meeting. He really saved the situation.

Shane and I got to know each other better over the last couple of days of the mission. He told me about two interesting trips he'd done. He'd built a raft and had gone down the Mekong, starting in China and continuing into Laos down to the southernmost part, as far as the river goes, into Thailand. It sounded like an amazing adventure. The other trip was on a motorbike, a Russian replica of a classic British motorbike. He'd driven all around China for the best part of three months.

Over a beer one evening, he told me a story about how he'd stopped to ask directions from a poor, ragged-looking guy. The man wanted a lift, so Shane asked him to take a seat in the sidecar and off they went to the man's village. When they got to the man's house, the man did what everyone does in China: he invited his visitor in. So in Shane went, into this tiny, simple hut, with a floor of dried mud. The man's grandmother was lying on the floor in the corner, very ill. Shane was offered a cup of tea – really just boiled water, because the family was so poor they had nothing to put into it. Shane said how frustrated he felt, seeing how desperately poor they were. He wanted to do something, anything, to help in some way. He just didn't know what to do. He thought of offering the man money, but it felt too awkward. What else could he do? After a short time, he thanked the man for his hospitality, and left him and his grandmother in their little shack. He felt sad and deeply frustrated.

A couple of weeks later, Shane got talking to another man who told him he was working on a project in a village about an hour's drive away. The man suggested that he and Shane could visit it together the next day. Shane rode his motorbike there and reckoned it must have been seventy or eighty kilometres away, over rough dirt roads. The project turned out to be a microfinance project, and Shane learned for the first time about savings and loans, and about small business development. He thought about the man he'd met a couple of weeks before.

He told me, 'I wondered whether that man – if he was given access to savings and loans, and some training – could set himself up in business.'

Microfinance offered a solution to that man's poverty in a way that would make him an equal in the transaction. Through savings, the man would be able to accumulate wealth, and a loan would enable him to build his business. It would be sustainable. For Shane, it was as though a light had been switched on. He became passionately interested in microfinance. He started a master's degree by correspondence through RMIT (Royal Melbourne Institute of Technology), focusing on microfinance. While working on the China program at AusAID in Beijing, he managed to get involved in the microfinance project with the Agricultural Bank of China.

While I was still there in Beijing waiting for the South African Embassy to issue my temporary passport, Shane got hold of my CV. He saw that I'd worked with FINCA Uganda and on microfinance projects managed by World Education. After that, he asked me lots of questions about the work I'd been doing, both in Uganda and as a consultant after I moved to Australia. Then I told him about setting up World Education Australia. He was clearly very interested.

Shortly before I left Beijing, Shane told me he had plans to leave AusAID. He and his partner, Junko, were planning to get married and come back to Australia. He'd been away from Australia for five or six years at that stage, mainly in Japan, where Junko was from, and in China.

A day or two before I was due to leave, I asked him, 'Hey, how about coming and working with me?'

One of the things that I've always been conscious of when you're looking to take someone on – whether as a member of your board or as part of your management team – is that there's the risk of hiring someone who thinks like you and who acts like you. If you do that, you're simply trying to replicate yourself. Of course, if you've got no faults, then that's a good thing! But for the rest of us, having someone that thinks and acts like you won't bring new strengths to your organisation. You need someone who will complement your own strengths, not duplicate them. Even after only knowing Shane for a couple of weeks, I was conscious that he approached things differently from me. Shane is more measured in his thinking than I am, more analytical. He tastes his food before he adds sugar or salt. I felt that he and I would complement each other.

If World Education Australia was going to grow, I knew I would need to take on more staff, but at that time we had very limited financial resources. Taking on another person was a risk. Shane told me he was planning to quit AusAID anyway, and he didn't yet have a job to go to when he moved back to Australia. By coming to work with me, I felt he'd be taking less of a risk than, say, someone who was already employed. If things didn't work out with World Education, then at least Shane wouldn't have sacrificed so much.

I made it clear that if he agreed to work with me, he'd need to live in Sydney. It was important, I thought, that we got to know each other better by working together. It wouldn't have worked, each of us living in different cities. Shane didn't have any intention of moving to Sydney at that time; his family were in Melbourne, and that's where he and Junko were planning to settle. But based on his experience of working with me over the previous couple of weeks, he gave the idea serious thought. Later, he told me that it hadn't taken him long to make up his mind.

Shane recalls, 'I don't know how long I thought about it. Maybe a day or two. Not long. The couple of weeks I'd spent working and travelling with Guy had been genuinely enjoyable, as well as intellectually stimulating. I could see that he had real rapport with people – with people in the villages, especially. I loved the way he used humour to engage people. But as well as being enjoyable, that time we spent together was hard work. It was clear to me that Guy is someone who works incredibly hard and expects the same from his team. Some people just bring part of themselves to a job, but Guy brings the whole of himself to his work. That resonated with me. And the idea of being part of a start-up appealed to my sense of adventure. It felt really exciting. So I thought, why not give it a go?'

Shane became the third staff member of World Education Australia, joining me and an office manager in our first office in Albert Avenue, in Chatswood, northern Sydney. The office had been a little two-bedroom unit in what was previously an old apartment block. It was fairly snug, with just two small offices: one was mine and the other was Shane's, which he shared with our volunteers. We also had a meeting room which would've previously been a living room. One of our volunteers, Diane Bowles, who joined World Education in the early years, had a baby son, Max. She didn't know what to do with him while she was working, as she didn't have childcare. I told her to bring him into work and leave him in my office – so she did! Max would sit on the floor beside my desk, happily playing with his toys and chortling away.

It was a busy time. I was doing a lot of consulting work, travelling much of the time. I more than covered my salary. Then I got Shane to take on consultancies as well, and that meant we could cover his salary too. Sometimes I'd win consulting assignments where I could expand the microfinance component to include a role for World Education. Shane would then come on board as a project team member. He and I were a good team.

∞

Under the Australian government's international aid program, Australian NGOs may be eligible for government funding. The amount of funding you receive from the government is determined by the level of contributions that you receive from the Australian public. The more you get from the Australian public, the more you have access to the pool of funds available under the Australian NGO Cooperation Program – which, in 2017, amounted to about $125 million a year.

But there's a catch. To be eligible for funding, you have to receive formal accreditation. To be accredited under the Australian NGO Cooperation Program, you have to have raised a minimum of $60,000 in community contributions, and you have to have minimum of two staff. These are two of the most important requirements; there are many others. All these requirements meant that we couldn't apply for the accreditation until we'd raised the money, and we couldn't raise the money until we'd got tax deductibility in the form of gift deductible recipient (GDR) status. We succeeded in getting GDR status in 2005, and then we started raising money as public donations. We first approached family and friends, asking for donations. One of the first big donations in that first year, after we got the tax deductibility status, was from a woman in Mittagong. She'd heard about us through her financial adviser, and she gave us $75,000! It was amazing. She didn't want to talk to us, or us to contact her, so we couldn't thank her directly. I don't know why she chose to donate to us; perhaps she simply thought we were doing a good job. Anyway, that was very generous. I remember thinking this fundraising gig is easy!

Up until about 2006, Shane and I relied heavily on consulting work to keep afloat, and we were away from home for much of the year. That was hard on Jacqui and Junko. We were also working hard on getting accreditation under the Australian NGO Cooperation Program. The following year we hired a consultant to help us finalise our application. She told us we weren't nearly ready and that if we submitted an application then, we wouldn't succeed in getting accreditation. So we stalled the application for another year.

The biggest issue for us when we started was that we were a consulting firm. Although we were a not-for-profit organisation, we were still a consulting firm. One of the requirements for accreditation under the Australian NGO Cooperation Program was that you needed a track record of managing projects for a minimum of two years. We didn't have that two-year track record. We were starting to manage projects and we were working with consulting firms to manage projects, but we didn't have years of managing projects on our own.

We also needed to be able to demonstrate a track record in fundraising. AusAID stipulated you had to raise a minimum of $60,000 per year, on average, over three years. Once you were accredited under the Australian NGO Cooperation Program, you qualified for government funding at a level that broadly matched the amount you spent each year on development projects – the annual recognised development expenditure (RDE). In the first year, we raised between $80,000 and $100,000, so we met the minimum requirement for public donations in that year. But it doesn't look good if you apply for funding from the government after raising the required level of public contributions for just one year.

The consultant we hired advised us, 'Look, it isn't a deal breaker, that particular issue, but the optics aren't good. Wait another year. You'll have to wait another year anyway to meet the requirements for project management.'

So we did, and by 2008 we'd had three consecutive years of raising more than $60,000 per year.

In 2009, when we finally succeeded in getting accreditation, AusAID told us that we'd only just made it over the line. There are two levels of accreditation: base and full. We were granted accreditation at the base level. Three years later, we succeeded in getting full accreditation. Essentially the criteria for the two levels are the same, but full accreditation requires you to demonstrate higher standards of management and monitoring of your projects. The biggest difference is that with base accreditation, you're entitled to up to $150,000 in government funding a year, whereas if you have full accreditation, you can get much more money. In 2017, we received around $700,000 in government funding.

The Australian NGO Cooperation Program is generally a good scheme. It certainly helped us to grow. There were about thirty accredited NGO aid agencies in 2009; now there are about forty. The accreditation process itself is pretty onerous. I guess the process ensures the government only works with a limited number of organisations who meet their requirements, partly because they have only a limited pool of funds to distribute, and partly to make the program more manageable. But I think the main reason they make the accreditation process difficult is that it raises the standards of operation for Australian NGOs. It definitely fosters best practice; it certainly did for us. We already had very good technical practices, but it helped us to round out our governance systems and our monitoring and evaluation. It forced us to do that.

∞

One project we were working on at that time was in Sri Lanka, funded by AusAID. It was a natural resource management project, working with the Department of Forestry in Colombo. The project was supporting poor rural communities around Sri Lanka, helping them to understand the importance of protecting the remaining remnants of natural forest around their villages. The real key to success was helping subsistence farmers to develop alternative livelihoods, so that instead of destroying the forest to make more land available for agriculture, the project gave them the means to diversify into small businesses.

My role as the microfinance specialist was to set up small savings and loans groups in the villages to help finance these new small business ventures. But the problem with this approach was that it was unlikely to be sustainable. We needed to find a way of connecting these poor communities up with local microfinance institutions in Sri Lanka. Of course, the microfinance institutions themselves – small banks and so on – weren't interested in taking on poor rural people as clients, because they had no savings and no assets. Many communities were remote, often made up of ethnic minorities that the banks didn't know or trust. The risks for the institutions were too high. We had to find a way of reducing those risks.

The way it worked was this. First, I managed to convince AusAID to include a new element in the project: guarantees. In essence that meant that some funds were put aside as guarantees in case people defaulted on their loans. I then managed to persuade seven microfinance institutions to partner with us. I told them, 'We'll reduce the risk for you. We'll provide guarantees against any losses you incur.' We agreed to cover fifty per cent of any losses in the first year, thirty-five per cent in the second year, and twenty per cent in the third year. We also paid for some motorbikes and basic infrastructure as an incentive to these microfinance institutions to expand their operations into these remote rural areas. In the end, we hardly spent any of the guarantee funds because the repayment rates on the small loans were so high. We only spent $1,000 or $2,000, something like that. It was negligible. And we ended up with all seven microfinance institutions setting up operations in thousands of villages, at very little cost to the Australian government. That was a sustainable model.

Shane and I worked hard on that project in Sri Lanka, but we also had a lot of fun. About twelve years ago, we were visiting a village to meet some of the members of a savings and loans group. We were waiting for the group to assemble, and we noticed a few local kids – ten or eleven-year-olds, that kind of age – playing cricket with a stick and a tennis ball. I started chatting to them, and they asked me where we were from. We told them we're from South Africa and Australia. Well, of course, that was it! These young kids invited us to play, and we ended up having an Australia versus Sri Lanka international test series with this bunch of eleven-year-old kids in a remote village in Sri Lanka. Those were the days of Shane Warne, so when Shane told them his name, the kids kept calling out 'Shane Warne, Shane Warne!' Sri Lanka definitely won that one. We got walloped!

A few years later, one of the local Sri Lankan staff I'd employed on that project came to Australia on holiday with his family. He told me that as far as he knew, from discussions with the Forestry Department and other contacts, the only part of that project that remained was the savings and loans groups and the livelihood development work. Of course, the Forestry Department staff still had the skills they'd learned from training courses they'd received through the project, but nothing else remained. It's interesting. All that money that AusAID invested in that project, and the only part of it still in evidence was the work we had done in microfinance. It was ironic, really, because in terms of the cost, the microfinance component was only a very small part of the overall investment.

∞

Consultancies were our bread and butter for the first few years, but public donations became an increasingly important source of revenue. I spent a lot of my time going to talk to foundations and companies, telling them about the work of World Education Australia and trying to persuade them to support us. I became conscious of the importance of the board's contacts. I started recruiting people onto the board from the corporate sector. I always liked that story about Jesse James, the legendary American outlaw in the 1800s. The story goes something like this: someone once asked Jesse, 'Hey, Jesse, why d'you rob banks?', to which Jesse replied, 'Well, that's where the money is!'

From about 2006, we started holding minor fundraising events. They weren't very well managed to start with; they were a bit amateurish, to be honest. But they had certain appeal, too; a certain authenticity. We didn't just look like a slick marketing set-up. I'd give a talk, our chair would give a talk, and then we'd ask people to sign up. We started raising money and we used that money to manage our own projects in countries like Nepal, Cambodia and Vietnam. We've grown from there. The last event we held was at The Establishment in George Street, Sydney: it was magnificent.

But raising funds is hard. Trying to get people to sign up to monthly contributions: that's the key to ensuring a guaranteed income stream. Some agencies hire marketing firms. We didn't do that. We did it all ourselves, with our volunteers. No commission was paid. We grew by fundraising; in recent years it's been our main source of revenue. But by about 2009 I was getting dissatisfied, partly from wearing out all those shoes and partly from telling the same story to the same people, over and over again, and listening to them say things to me like, 'But why are you spending fifteen per cent of the money I gave you on administration?', or 'I bank with Westpac. They could provide banking services in Laos. You should just tell Westpac to go and work in Laos.' Sure, why not? If only it was that easy!

It was all very frustrating. You raise the money; you spend it as best you can; you build up your program. And then you go back to the same donors and tell them the same story... It's a real treadmill. You start to wonder how much of what you're doing is for the funders and how much is for poor communities. We'd always try to approach the community first, assess their needs and develop a program from there. But sometimes a potential donor would say something like, 'You should go and do some work in Tonga. I was there on holiday and I really like the place. I'll give you $50,000 if you go to Tonga and run a program there.' Believe it or not, that's a true story! It was frustrating, trying to explain to people why we couldn't simply do what they were suggesting.

I started looking for a different way to work. I wanted to get off the treadmill. I wanted to find a business model that would provide more annuity income, if you like; more of an income stream. That's where the idea of an online lending platform began: a facility that would enable someone in Australia or another First World country to lend directly to someone in the developing world – Nepal, Vietnam, Papua New Guinea – anywhere that we were working. The idea had huge potential.

All we had to do was make it happen.

# 9

# In the field

*If speaking is silver, then listening is gold – Turkish proverb*

On the kitchen wall in the Winship family home there's a framed photograph of Guy with a group of women, dated 17th August 2006. The photograph is slightly faded, sepia-tinted, and made to look like it was taken many decades ago. Guy, seated in the front, is wearing a garland of flowers and a big grin. Behind and around him are about twenty-five women dressed in saris. One is holding a baby on her lap. Most are smiling as broadly as Guy. Below the photograph, there's a small brass plate which reads,

> Guy Winship, Founder & CEO, WEAL, 2003–2016
> Our world is a better place because of your vision, spirit and humanity.
> Thank you.

That photo was taken on a hillside in a remote village in north-western Nepal. The women in the picture were members of a savings and loans group which had been formed in 1998 by the team at World Education Nepal. About once a year I'd visit the villages where we were working, travelling with two or three staff members: the project manager from the World Education office in Kathmandu, Lotika Paintal, and a couple of field coordinators, Lakshmi and Ramchandra Khanal.

On this particular occasion, when the photograph was taken, we'd driven for about an hour from the nearest town to visit this village. The savings group called itself Utt Prahana and the members were running a small business, growing and selling spices. They would dry the spices and then grind them by hand to sell in the local market. They wanted

*Guy with members of a savings and loans group, Arghakhanchi district, north-western Nepal, 2007.*

an electric-powered machine with a generator so that they could grind larger quantities of spices much more quickly, and they asked me for the money to buy one.

The group was formed under a project funded by USAID, the Resunga Mahila Karyakram project. Resunga Mahila is the name of a sacred mountain in Nepal, and karyakram means 'program' or 'project' in Nepalese. The Resunga Mahila Karyakram project was working in villages in two districts in the west of Nepal, Gulmi and Arghakhanchi. World Education Nepal managed the project, and they'd established savings and loans groups in each village. The members would save money amongst themselves, and then when one of them wanted a loan, the group would lend part of their savings to that person. It was all based on trust, knowing each other well: they were all friends and neighbours, and some were related to each other. Mutual trust was the fundamental dynamic that made the scheme work.

These villages were incredibly remote. We'd fly from Kathmandu to Bhairahawa in western Nepal. Bhairahawa is only about twenty kilometres from Lumbini, the birthplace of Buddha, so the area attracts

*Guy with villagers, Arghakhanchi district, north-western Nepal, 2007.*

a lot of Buddhist pilgrims and tourists. Bhairahawa is also one of the main gateways into Nepal for overland travellers and backpackers. We'd drive north from Bhairahawa into the mountains for about five hours along narrow, twisting roads cut into the side of the mountain. A real challenge for me, given my fear of heights! It probably wasn't that far – maybe no more than a hundred kilometres – but you couldn't drive at more than twenty or thirty kilometres an hour because the roads were so bad. I'd spend most of those four or five hours in a state of white-knuckled terror, wondering if we'd make it or if we'd end up at the bottom of a ravine. A bus would appear around a bend and there'd be only enough room for one vehicle, so one of us would have to stop and back up to where there was enough room for two vehicles to pass each other. Reversing downhill on a narrow, twisting dirt road, with the mountain on one side and a precipice on the other, was no joke. Sometimes you'd start backing up, with the bus ahead of you, impatient to pass, and you'd see another car or truck appear behind you – and there'd be nowhere to go! More than once I'd pull in as close as possible to the side of the mountain and then jump out and press myself against the mountainside to let the bus go by.

After driving like that for four or five hours, we'd stay overnight in Gulmi or Argakhanchi, the district capitals. They're both very small and remote. I remember staying in a sort of rest house there, where they gave me the best room in the place for the princely sum of about $12. I had the room to myself, complete with single bed, a battered old chest of drawers, and bedbugs. I ended up sleeping on top of the bed sheet to avoid being bitten. I couldn't read after dark because the light from the single bulb hanging from the ceiling was too feeble. I didn't want to use my laptop because the power supply was unreliable and I was also worried about the voltage. Dinner was served in a communal eating area: lentil dahl and rice. Breakfast was the same. That was the staple food, wherever you went, for breakfast, lunch and dinner. If you were lucky, there might be a bit of chicken in it. My team mates, Lokita, Lakshmi and Ramchandra, took it all in their stride, and I wanted to do the same myself.

The next morning we'd drive to the bottom of the mountain, which is as close as you can get to the villages where we were due to meet with the groups. From there, we'd walk for two or three hours along rough mountain paths, passing herds of yak and occasionally a few villagers. We sometimes saw women and men carrying immense loads of straw or firewood in baskets on their backs, with a strap around their forehead. As we approached a village, the first people we'd see would be the children. They'd come running up and touch me on the arm or the hand and chatter away excitedly in Nepalese, and then they'd laugh and run away and tell their parents that a white man was coming. I'd see the women appearing, coming out of their houses one by one, and then everyone would gather, usually in the market place or another meeting place, and wait for me to arrive. It was seen very much as a women's meeting. None of the men would come. Many of the women brought their children with them to the meeting, babies and toddlers who'd cling to their mothers' saris, peering shyly at the white stranger.

In that photograph of me with the group of Nepalese women, there's a dark smudge on my forehead. That was a tika, a red dot of vermilion paste traditionally made from dried cinnabar, turmeric and water. The women applied a tika to my forehead as a blessing and a sign of welcome, and they put a garland of sweet-smelling flowers around my neck. It was extraordinarily moving, the way these women welcomed me so warmly.

When everyone had arrived, the village chief would make a little speech of welcome, followed by a speech by a local government official, and then I'd reply. I often wondered what went on in the minds of these women as they listened to these speeches; what they thought about me and about Australia. I would always ask the women about their lives: how many children they had, how long they'd been with the group, what the group did for them. I'd ask them about the challenges they'd faced in setting up and running the group; what had been the problems and what had been the successes. I would talk to the women about their aspirations and their hopes for the future. A few of the women could speak a little English, and that was a great advantage. That was often not the case in other countries where we were working, for example in Cambodia, or in Laos. There's much less English spoken there, whereas in Nepal – I guess because of its history – I could engage directly with some of the women. Otherwise, I'd need to work through an interpreter.

Although they lived in this incredibly remote rural village up in the mountains in the west of Nepal, the women's aspirations and hopes were so similar to our own in our society. They would always mention their children: how they hoped that their children would get an education and have better life than they could. They would say if they could work hard and make more money, then they could help their children more. I always found that very moving.

Then I'd ask them to ask me questions. They would be a little shy at first, unsure whether to speak up in that public gathering. Then they'd gradually gain confidence and start asking me about my family – 'How many children do you have?' and 'What does your wife look like?', that kind of thing. I always used to carry a picture of Jacqui and the kids with me, but that wasn't much to show them. Since having a smartphone, I've been able to show the women lots of photographs of life at home, so they could form a better picture of my life and my family. The women would ask me about Australia, and they'd ask about getting on a plane. None of them had ever been on a plane; I told them that it's like being on a bus, but unlike most buses in Nepal, I told them, there's a toilet at the back of the plane, and you get a package meal. But just like being on a bus, sometimes the plane bounces a little, like when you're driving along on a dirt road, and sometimes it's smooth, like when you're on a sealed road.

But try to explain what life is like in Sydney to people who have never been beyond Kathmandu! This particular group would've been to Kathmandu a few times, including for training workshops run by World Education Nepal. Getting to Kathmandu once or twice a year is a really big deal for those women. The thought of how far away Australia is would've been beyond their wildest imaginings. I don't think that community had access to television – at least, I didn't see any. One of the problems in Nepal is electricity; they can have blackouts for days, even in the middle of Kathmandu, and solar doesn't work well up in the mountains because many of the valleys are so deep they're in perpetual shadow. Some villages have power from micro-hydro plants, but I didn't see any evidence of that in this particular village.

The women often asked me for money. They probably thought I was very wealthy, and of course it's true that I have much, much more money than they do. I often thought to myself, I can't help all these people. I felt a bit helpless, not being able to help them directly. But it's not really appropriate to hand out a bit of cash: the work we're doing is meant to be sustainable and not just welfare handouts. It made me think about my own fundraising work, and about my relationship with the wealthy Australians I would approach for donations. And then I'd think about these poor village women, asking me for a few hundred dollars to buy a spice-grinding machine and a generator. It seemed to complete the circle: me asking for money from wealthy Australians, and these women asking me for money.

I've always enjoyed meeting the people that we're helping. It's grounding; it brings a new appreciation. It reminds me how fortunate I have been materially. Visiting the groups and talking to the beneficiaries is good for my soul. It makes me feel good that people need and appreciate the services that we give. Coming back to Australia, you appreciate how well off you are, with our health services, our education services, our material wealth. We live in an increasingly consumer-focused, materialistic society. We push and push to get more money, push and push to acquire more things. But it doesn't make you happier. The smiles and laughter of these poor rural women was a sharp reminder that life isn't all about money. I saw how happy some of them appeared to be, with so much less: a much simpler lifestyle than our own. Basic houses, with floors of packed earth. No mobile phones, no television. Talking to these women and spending a few hours with them in their remote mountain village made me rethink my values, re-evaluate my beliefs. It also reinforced my commitment to finding ways to help them improve their lives and the lives of their children.

∞

On one of my trips to Nepal, I met a group of Maoists, young guys aged around sixteen or seventeen, at a textile factory on the outskirts of Kathmandu. The factory employed a number of young girls, and one of the projects that we were working on was aimed at addressing child labour and people trafficking. The project was sponsored by the US Department of Labor to try to get children and young people out of bad workplaces. The project was also trying to stop sex trafficking, where young adolescents – some of them only children – were being sent overseas to work in the sex industry, but mainly the project focused on child labour. My role on the project was as an advisor on microfinance.

Working on projects to end child labour is challenging. If we were simply to say to the owner or manager of the factory employing children, 'You've got to get this twelve-year-old kid out of here', what would happen to their families? Those children are contributing to their families' income; they may be supporting a sick parent or helping to save for their sister's wedding. The issue isn't straightforward, and finding a solution isn't easy. But one solution was to try to help the families to save, to learn to put a little money aside each week, so they became less dependent on their children to contribute to the family income.

We were due to meet a savings and loans group whose members were women employed at the factory. The group had been organised by Maoists: they were quite open about it. The Maoists had a really significant following during the civil conflict. They were very popular; they'd won around forty per cent of the vote in the elections.

We met the women and gave them their savings passbooks and explained to them why savings are important. My Nepalese colleagues were doing the training; I was simply an observer. My role was to do the accounting, help set up the system, and prepare the operational manuals on how the savings group would work.

I got talking to this group of young Maoists. They were curious about me and asked me a lot of questions – 'What do you do in Australia? Where do you work?' – and I told them, 'You know, a lot of the work I do in Australia is actually like begging. It's not begging in the way that you think – sitting on the street with your hand out or a cap in front of you for people to throw a few coins in. We have to go and ask wealthy Australians and the Australian government for money so that we can come and do this work with you. That's where the money comes from.'

We had a really interesting discussion around what the role of government was and where the government gets its own funds from. That discussion was quite thought-provoking for me. Thought-provoking for these Maoists too, I imagine. It was pretty clear that they had the view that the way out of poverty was for the government simply to give people more money. They had the perception that the government has limitless money. They were quite militant in their views. That was quite confronting for me – not physically; I actually felt completely safe – but confronting in terms of my world view. A lot of the work that we do is around entrepreneurship, building up savings, helping people to start businesses – which of course is based on a capitalist paradigm. It's so different from the communist mindset, where the government gives you a job working in a factory or fixing roads or teaching in a school. Everything is organised by the government.

That meeting with the Maoists was interesting. I wouldn't say that I agreed with a lot of what they said, but I certainly felt challenged by the questions they asked. They opened my mind to new perspectives and a completely different way of thinking. That's true of many of the encounters we have with the groups we work with, talking to them, asking them about their lives, their families. It's not simply that we provide skills to them; they provide skills to us. Having one's world view challenged is healthy. That's why the work that we do teaches us as much as we teach others – maybe more! We have so much to learn from our beneficiaries. They may not have a lot of formal education, but they're not ignorant. They have a lot of valuable life experience. We shouldn't assume that just because they're not educated they haven't got the skills to work in their own environment. That's why it's so important for us to understand the environment they're in so we can try to support them to work within that environment, rather than imposing a different way of working from outside.

∞

As in the poor rural areas of Nepal, in many of the poorest parts of Cambodia the lure of a regular income and the excitement of city life draws girls out of school and into the towns, often to work in garment factories. In a project known as OPTIONS, World Education worked on helping adolescent girls to stay in their villages with their families instead of working in garment factories in Phnom Penh. We worked in villages in some of the very poorest provinces in Cambodia, helping the girls to reintegrate into village life and resume their schooling.

The project also educated the girls and their families about the risks and consequences of sexual exploitation. I believe strongly in the value of education, but the truth is many of these families are extremely poor. Their children are an important source of family income; they can't afford not to send them out to work. They are under enormous economic pressure, and this pressure drives their decisions around educating their kids and sending them off to jobs in towns where they're exposed to exploitation. Typically, they'd send their daughters out to work and keep their sons at school. Someone might come into the village to recruit labour for a garment factory, and although a family might know that sending their daughter away to work as a factory worker could expose her to the risk of being pressured into prostitution, they needed the money. It's not straightforward. Getting girls out of situations where they might be exploited or abused is obviously ideal, but the grim reality for many poor families is that with the girl back at home, she's no longer contributing to the family income – and there's another mouth to feed.

I talked to one of the project managers, Estelle Day, about how we could help reduce the pressure on these families so that they wouldn't send their daughters away to work. Estelle then presented a case to the US Department of Labor. To address the sexual exploitation of girls, she argued, the project needed to address the problem of poverty. Until families have an alternative means of livelihood, they will continue to send their daughters away to work in the cities. The Department of Labor supported Estelle's case, and consequently we redesigned the project to include livelihood development and education. Then, as well as supporting the girls to return to their villages and finish their schooling, we taught them a trade and gave them the skills and the means to start a small business, like sewing or running a little shop. We managed that component over the next few years. I was proud of that project.

I remember one occasion when Shane and I travelled to Cambodia

*Shane facilitating a focus group discussion with villagers in Prey Veng, Cambodia, 2005.*

as part of our work on the OPTIONS project. We visited a village in Prey Veng, south-east of Phnom Penh, near the Vietnamese border, where we ran a series of training sessions in microfinance and livelihood development. A young woman in her late teens had returned to the village some months previously, and with support from the project had set herself up as a hairdresser. She had a small 'shop' in the marketplace: there was a little stool for her customers to sit on, an umbrella to provide a bit of shade, and a small mirror attached to the side of one of the market stalls. We got chatting to this young woman, asking her about her business and how it was going.

Then I said, 'Okay, why don't you give me a haircut?'

She thought I was joking. She looked at me and said, 'Oh no, I can't! I don't know what to do with your hair. I've never cut that kind of hair before.'

I said, 'No, I'm serious!'

After a bit of persuading, the young woman reluctantly agreed, and I took a seat on the little stool. A small crowd started to gather. It was quite a novelty, watching this white foreigner getting a haircut!

*Shane with participants in the OPTIONS project, Prey Veng, Cambodia, 2005.*

Shane recalls that when the young woman had finished cutting Guy's hair, she asked for the equivalent of about two dollars.

'Guy said, "You can't charge two dollars! That's far too little. I'll give you five dollars!"

She looked at him strangely. She probably thought he'd misunderstand her, or maybe he was just a bit stupid, and she said, "I said two dollars."

And Guy replied, "No, no! You've got to haggle with me."

She repeated that he owed just two dollars, and Guy shrugged and said, "Okay, then, four dollars!"

Eventually they agreed on three, but I think Guy gave her five dollars anyway. She and the onlookers all thought it was hilarious. She said it was the first time a customer had argued with her that they should pay more!'

∞

Working in international development, in the NGO sector, I've often felt squeezed between the people who fund our work and the communities we work with. The funders want you to do one thing, and the communities you work with want you to do another. Some of our funders come up with quite simplistic solutions. They may be successful in business, but that doesn't make them experts in the causes of poverty. 'We'll give you the money,' they say to us, 'if you go and tell those people that they must have fewer children.' A Queensland farmer actually said that to me once.

It's particularly challenging when you're designing projects, trying to meet the requirements of the funders and to fit what you want to do into their boxes, and working with the communities, with their limitations. Sometimes I've questioned the efficacy of what we're doing when we find ourselves squeezed between the funder and the beneficiary. That's essentially what happens. As an international NGO, World Education Australia is essentially an intermediary, working with both the funder and the beneficiary, trying to satisfy the needs of both. It can be very difficult, navigating your way between the two.

We worked on a social incomes project in Laos recently, funded by the Australian government, around social incomes. This was one of those projects where I've felt like I've been squeezed between what the funder wanted and what I knew to be better for the beneficiaries. There are a lot of poor communities in Laos, and this project focused on some of the very poorest communities in the southern part of the country. The project was based on a similar project in north-western Bangladesh, where cash and asset handouts had been provided to what they called the 'ultra-poor'. That project in Bangladesh had had some success at lifting people out of poverty, and the idea was to replicate this in Laos. So the Australian government designed the new project as a welfare project, providing these poor communities in Laos with asset transfers, like goats and seeds and a little income, to get them started on the path out of poverty. That was good in one sense: it did enable some people to increase their incomes in the short term. The problem,

*Guy visiting a rural community in Laos, 2010.*

though, was that it didn't teach people the skills they needed to lift themselves out of poverty over the longer term. Developing those skills takes time.

The other problem was that the Australian government designed the project largely without consulting with the Laos government. So when the project came to an end, that was that. The end of the deal. Some people in those very poor communities did okay, at least in the short term; those that were chosen to participate in this wealth transfer, they scored. But they were only a very few among many communities in that poor region in southern Laos. The other communities didn't benefit at all. It's like a lottery: some communities gained, and some didn't. I think that's really unfair. When I talked with the Laos government officials, they admitted that this project had been a one-off. 'We haven't got the money to do this again,' they told me. 'The project has been good, and these communities have benefitted, but we don't have the money to replicate this elsewhere.' Replication is really important. After the donor funding ends, it's important to make sure the project can continue to make a difference.

We tendered for part of the project, along with a couple of other

NGOs, and a big British consulting firm won some other parts of the project. Once the project design had been approved, the contracts awarded and the project was under way, the Australian government wasn't in a position to adjust the design. With some modifications, we could've done so much more to make the project more sustainable. When the project was reviewed about halfway through, a team of consultants came and evaluated what had been done against what was in the project design document, ticking off the outputs against the objectives and so on. We did pretty well, but we felt squeezed between the need to follow the processes set out in a poorly thought-out design and the little bit we could do to improve the outcomes. One small example of what we could have done is to set up a goat-rearing facility, which would have meant that they'd have been able to produce more goats every year, whereas the model that was set out in the design was that you just buy the goat and give it to the local villagers. These are the kind of small differences that would have made the whole thing more sustainable and more replicable.

The project was originally designed in three three-year phases. The consultants who did the feasibility study and put the project design together recognised the value of learning from experience. The plan was that we'd learn from each phase what worked and what didn't, and the lessons learned in the first three years could then be applied to the next three years. But the funding was cut after the first phase due to cuts to the government's aid budget, so whatever lessons had been learned from the first phase couldn't be applied. There wasn't time to change anything. All we could do was focus on what we were supposed to achieve in that first three-year phase. It took us most of the first year to get everything up and running, including hiring and training the staff, setting up the systems and so on – which is pretty typical for an international development project of that kind. Then with the project finishing at the end of that first three years, the staff began looking for other work well before the three years were up. Many left in the last six months, so it ended up in effect being an eighteen-month project.

When I met with the first secretary in AusAID at the Australian embassy in Vientiane, I talked to him about the time it takes to get a project up and running. He appreciated my points, but he had his own targets to meet. In terms of those targets, the time we'd taken to set up the project wasn't acceptable.

A few days later, I arrived back in Australia and caught a taxi home from the airport. On the back seat of the taxi there was a copy of the *Sydney Morning Herald*. I picked it up and read that it takes eighteen to twenty months to get a development application approved in Sydney for the construction of new block of apartments. It made me think about what the AusAID officer in the embassy in Laos had told me, that a year was too long to set up the project. Reading how long it takes to get a building project up and running in Sydney, I reflected on how much more challenging it is to get a project established in a developing country, a poor country where government systems are often weak and capacity is low. Good project designs take these constraints into account; poor designs set unrealistic goals in too-short time frames.

International development plays a valuable role in helping people to lift themselves out of poverty. A vital element of well-designed technical assistance projects is building people's skills and developing the capacity of local institutions so that change is sustainable in the long term. But there's only so much you can do. Running savings groups and training people in financial management doesn't change the big picture; it doesn't change a country's governance structure or the legal system. As an international development agency, we can't do that. Those big picture reforms are vitally important, but of course they're highly political. Designing those types of intervention involves making political judgements, and funders shy away from anything political. The more I think about the work we do, the more certain I am that if there was better governance and stronger civil society and democratic institutions in the countries where we work, we would be able to achieve so much more.

# 10

# The birth of Good Return

> 'Never doubt that a small group of thoughtful,
> committed citizens can change the world; indeed, it's
> the only thing that ever has' – Margaret Mead

Fundraising has been a huge part of my work with World Education Australia. I was wearing out my shoes going to talk to corporates and wealthy Australians. Shane and I were spreading ourselves increasingly thin, trying to balance our work on consultancies and projects with raising enough capital through donations to keep the whole thing ticking over. By 2006, I had started looking for a business model that would get me off the fundraising treadmill.

Fundraising is our cost of capital. The cost of capital is one of the biggest challenges that microfinance institutions face, and it's why a lot of them charge their customers very high interest rates. It's the reason why some microfinance programs fail. It boils down to the acquisition cost; it's really only worth investing a lot of time in talking to people who are going to give you a significant amount –more than $10,000, say. And that, of course, is why I focused on corporations and wealthy individuals. If I have to spend a lot of time selling the idea of what we do to someone, telling them why what we're doing is important, and how their money will be used to help people save or start a business, and that person ends up giving us $50, then it's just not worthwhile. It's not sustainable.

What we needed was a different way of working, a way to generate a sustainable income stream and reduce our cost of capital.

Around that time, I heard about Kiva, a non-profit organisation that was founded in San Francisco in 2005. Kiva runs an online lending scheme to connect lenders to people around the world who want to start small businesses. Later, I heard about another online fundraising program that a group had started in France. They came up with a scheme called Baby Loan, which provides small loans to people in Africa via an online mechanism.

The idea of raising money online got me thinking. This could be the key to generating income while keeping the acquisition cost low. It seemed to me that we could set up something like that here in Australia: an online lending scheme in which Australians could donate or lend to poor people in Asia or the Pacific or in remote rural Australia. We could raise capital from the Australian public at zero per cent interest and pass it on to our partner banks, our partner microfinance agencies, at zero per cent interest, at very little administration cost. That would mean our partners could charge lower interest rates – and so benefit their clients.

Shane and I contacted the president of Kiva. We talked to him about their online lending program and our own plans to launch a similar type of program in Australia. The president sounded interested. He said he was willing to help us – at a cost, of course! – but would need to get the approval of his board. He quoted me US$50,000 for the software. Shane and I thought it over and decided that we could manage US$50,000. We got back in touch with Kiva and said we'd like to go ahead.

The president of Kiva talked to his board and then got back to us. 'The board says yes,' he told us. 'We'd like to help you set up in Australia, but it's going to cost you US$500,000.' That was just for access to the software!

We sat down and talked it over, but US$500,000 was way beyond our means. We just didn't have the money. For vastly less than that, we thought we could develop our own software, design it ourselves, set it up exactly as we wanted it, and not need approval from San Francisco. Shane has more IT knowledge than me, but neither of us knew enough about how to do the programming, how much it would cost, how long it would take and the intricacies of the tech side.

We had a smart young guy working with us at that time as a volunteer, James Le Compte, who had started his own software company while he was at university doing his master's. We talked to James about our proposal; he agreed to work pro bono to get the project started, and once we started raising money then we would pay him. That seemed like a good deal, and we agreed. James put together a business plan while Shane and I continued to try and raise funds.

One day, James was visiting his mate Neil Cairns at Neil's parents' place. Over a coffee in the kitchen, James told Neil and his father, Gordon Cairns, about the project. 'I'm working on this loan scheme,' James told them. 'We're trying to put together an online lending program that will enable Australians to lend money to people in poor countries. You'll be able to go online and choose who you want to lend money to.'

Gordon was really interested. He told James that he'd 'really like to meet the people behind this scheme'. He got in touch with me and arranged to meet me at the office.

Gordon Cairns is today the chairman of Woolworths and the chairman of Origin Energy. He was then on the board of Westpac. He's very easily the number one company director in Australia. He arrived at our little two-room office in Chatswood and looked around. He was clearly unimpressed. Then he looked at me and said, in his broad Scottish accent, 'I don't know you. I don't know if I want to give you my support.' Very blunt!

And I replied, quick as a flash, 'I don't know you either. I don't know if I should accept your support!'

And Gordon just burst out laughing. It was the start of a special friendship between us. Mind you, Gordon still did his homework on us. He hired a consultant to do a due diligence on us.

We held a fundraising event around that time, while we were developing the online lending program. Gordon made a generous donation himself, and he also introduced us to Westpac, who gave us around $300,000 to cover the development of the online lending program. It took us a year to get the program up and running: the lending mechanism, the website, all the IT processes. It ended up costing us a whole lot more than we bargained for and it took much longer than we had planned.

We launched the program under the name Good Return, and the website went live to the public in April 2010. Good Return became our individual giving program: members of the public could choose either to give a loan and get their money back when the loan was repaid, or they could donate the loan. If they choose to donate the money once the beneficiary has repaid their loan, then the money comes back to us as a donation. We can then use that money to support our education programs.

At first, we just used Good Return as a trading name, but because we wanted to direct people to the Good Return website to make loans and donations and give us that income stream, we eventually decided to use the name Good Return for everything we do. We explain to corporates that we're actually World Education Australia trading as Good Return, and that while Good Return consists of the online loans scheme, it also consists of all the other programs we run. With a corporate donor, we can invest time in explaining how it all works. Individual givers who donate $50 or $100 can look on our website to find out all about us and our work. A lot of people just know us as a loans scheme and nothing else.

Although we've changed our name, we're still World Education Australia, and we still have the same affiliation with World Education Incorporated in Boston. We still have a close relationship with them. They agreed to the name change; they understood that it would work better for us. They are our founding member, which gives them certain rights, including the right to appoint up to two directors. We have ten directors at the moment, with two appointed by Boston: myself and James McNeil, the new vice president of World Education's Asia

Division. Interestingly, as an aside, one of the reasons that I'm a director is that World Education didn't know who else to appoint as directors other than me and David Kahler. I remain a director representing World Education Inc. It's unusual in the NGO sector in Australia and among international NGOs for the CEO to be a director, but World Education Inc. were happy enough with the services I'd provided them in the past, I guess, and felt confident enough for me to represent them on the board.

Our online lending program generates some income for us, but only very little. All up, it accounts for about two per cent of our income. The amount that's coming in as repayable loans is quite significant – I think a total of about $500,000 last year – but that doesn't go into our income statement because we don't get the money. All of that money goes out to our partners to distribute to the beneficiaries. We clip the ticket by charging a fee for each loan: the minimum is $5 on small loans, and the maximum is $25. If someone makes a loan of $1,000, we charge two-and-a-half per cent. If people are making loans of $2,000, $5,000 or $10,000, we charge a $25 fee per loan. We don't generate much income from the turnover; I can't remember the exact figures, but last year we earned maybe $30,000 in loan fees out of a turnover of $3.5 million. Not much at all. It's donations that generate income for us – that's when people decide to give their loan as a donation. That's where we get an income stream. Overall, in terms of volume, about a quarter of loans are made as donations. The rest are straight loans, where the lender is repaid.

∞

The founding directors of World Education Australia, which has been trading as Good Return since 2010, were David Kahler, Pam Jonas, and myself.

David Kahler was vice president of World Education in Boston: a remarkably intelligent, hard-working and committed development

*David Kahler, Guy, Pam Jonas and Shane Nichols at the World Education regional meeting in Siem Reap, Cambodia, 2005.*

worker, although he had little patience for those who couldn't keep up with him. David and I became very close, and it was a shock when I heard he'd been diagnosed with leukaemia in around 2010. He retired to France and passed away in September 2015, just a few months after we'd had lunch together in Paris.

James MacNeil has worked for World Education Inc. on education and livelihood development programs in Indonesia, Cambodia, Nepal and India. He's based in Boston, where he is vice president of World Education's Asia Division, and he replaced David as the World Education Inc. representative on our board.

The third founding director of World Education Australia, Pam Jonas, and our founding chair, was recommended by David Kahler. Pam has worked for more than three decades in education and training, and on employment policy. She now splits her time between Australia and France. Pam and her husband Frank have become close friends of Jacqui's and mine, and they often stay with us when they are in Sydney attending board meetings or functions. Pam retired as chair in 2010, but she's still on the board. She has been a great contributor in terms of managing and steering the organisation.

It was just the three of us for about two years, and then we started gradually growing the board. The other members joined through various networks and contacts, and sometimes through our donor organisations. Each of them has made a major contribution, and all of them have become personal friends of mine. They are a critical factor in the success of Good Return.

I met Neild McIntosh through a mutual friend who he was doing some work for. Neild was an actuary by profession before joining the family business, Austral Engineering. The company went public in about 2000, enabling Neild to retire and undertake a master's in international development at the University of New South Wales. I met him in 2003, as he was finishing his degree, when he was volunteering in a soup kitchen.

I said to him, 'You're doing a great job, Neild – and I'm sure your soup is delicious! – but you're an actuary and an experienced business executive. You have incredible skills in the finance sector. With your experience and your degree in international development, you could do so much more. Come and work with us!'

Neild started as a volunteer before joining the board. In 2010 he stepped up as chair after Pam resigned, and he had to endure a trip to Boston with me. He claims I told everyone we met on that trip about Good Return! Neild and his family have been incredibly generous to us. They were the inaugural funders of the World Education Australia Aid Trust Fund and have continued to be a generous donor ever since.

Gordon Cairns has been on the board of Good Return now for eight years. He's a great listener and he's as sharp as a razor blade. He's very strategic. At board meetings, he cuts straight to the chase. I'll have written five pages analysing a problem and all the possible solutions. I'll present the paper to the board and I'll say, 'This is the problem and these are the possible solutions. I think we should do this.' Everyone chats away and we discuss the options. Then they'll turn to Gordon and ask him, 'So, Gordon, what do you think?' and he'll say, 'So this is the problem? Okay, then this is the solution. Let's do that.' He synthesises the issues down to the essentials. He has a mind like a machine. But he's also warm and generous, and he's become a very good friend.

When I knew that I was about to have my eye out, I phoned all my board members. I rang Gordon and said, 'I've got cancer. I'm going to have my eye removed. I'll be off for a month.' He was very sympathetic. And then a year after that, I phoned all the board and told them that the cancer had metastasised and that it was terminal. In his usual direct way, Gordon asked me, 'So, how long have you got?' Like I said, he cuts to the chase. No one else asked me that question. I didn't actually answer him directly; I was struggling with coming to terms with the diagnosis at that time. Telling him would have made it too real.

∞

Our largest donor to date has been Accenture, a major professional services company. They've been giving us roughly $300,000 each year since about 2013. Damian Woods, who was one of their senior partners and a board member of the Accenture Foundation, joined our board in about 2012. Damian is known for his quick wit and dapper charm, but he's also extremely smart and a really hard worker who has been an asset to Good Return.

Origin Energy has been another major donor. When Gordon became their chairman, they made a $50 million endowment in the newly-established Origin Foundation. Good Return was one of the first recipients from that foundation. Of course, Gordon was on our board by then, and a very strong supporter.

Then there's Clayton Utz, a prominent law firm with offices in Sydney. Initially, my cousin, David Alexander, had very kindly been providing us with pro bono legal services. However, Neild had a contact at Clayton Utz and, through that contact, Clayton Utz then offered us pro bono support and some donated funds. Kate Jordan is one of the two deputy chief executive partners at Clayton Utz. She's been the chair of our board for the last two years and recently became our deputy CEO, looking after the people and recruitment side of things. She is a brilliant lawyer with a strong grasp of governance and business, great ethics and, most of all, a heart of gold.

There's a story behind every director. Take William Pigott, for example (or Bill, as we know him). A lovely guy. I met him through his son, Peter Pigott, who volunteered with World Education in Cambodia. Bill is a retired doctor who worked for the World Health Organisation (WHO) for twenty-one years. Before he retired, Bill was the WHO country representative in Cambodia and Nepal, also teaching at the UN Medical School in Geneva. He understood development and education, although more from a health perspective than from a livelihoods perspective. As an international development NGO, we need people with solid development experience on our board. I'd succeeded in bringing in people from the corporate sector; that was important to raise our profile and build the networks which are obviously vital for helping us to generate funding. But we needed development people, and with his WHO experience and many years working in Asia, Bill was just the right kind of guy. He joined the board in about 2006 and is still a member today. He has been very emotionally supportive of me with my cancer, keeping a candle burning for me in his home in Berry on the New South Wales south coast.

Margaret Wright was a contact of Gordon's, having interviewed him for her own book a few years previously. Margaret was an active board member from 2010 to 2015. A qualified accountant, she was the chair of the board's audit committee for a number of years. Her high-level IT skills proved extremely useful in the design and establishment of the Good Return online loans program. She and her husband Eric became good friends of mine over many long discussions around strategy and how to deal with operational IT issues without any resources! Margaret left the board to focus on her own business interests, but she remains a friend and a supporter of Good Return.

*Guy and members of the Good Return board visit a rural community in Prey Veng, Cambodia, March 2016.*

More recent board members include Sondra Cortis, the deputy chief financial officer for Westpac International; Sonia Higgins, who, along with her husband Steve, is also a well-known food blogger (which Jacqui found very intimidating when they came to our place for dinner!); and Joanna Ledgerwood, an old and special friend from Uganda days. Joanna is a former banker, a world expert in microfinance, and the author of several books on the subject.

∞

In April 2016, we organised a week-long trip to Cambodia for the board members. They all paid for themselves, and some of us with spouses and partners brought them along too. This was a special trip for me. It was the first time that Jacqui had accompanied me on a work trip, so she finally got to see for herself the kind of work I had been doing on all those long trips away from home.

We started in Phnom Penh and then visited villages in Prey Veng province, a very poor area in the south. We did day trips to the villages,

*Guy with members of the Good Return board outside the Royal Palace, Phnom Penh, Cambodia, March 2016. L to Rt: Frank Ward (Pam Jonas's husband); James MacNeil, director; Neild MacIntosh, director; Kate Jordan, board chair; Sondra Cortis, director; Tracy Woods (Damien Woods's wife); Damien Woods, director; Guy; Helena Hurley, Good Return Corporate Partnerships Manager; Edy Hartono, World Education Country Director for Indonesia.*

driving two or three hours to visit some of the more distant villages. The group saw for themselves the work we were doing there; we explained how the education program worked and how the loans scheme worked. We had meetings with our partners, the local NGOs and community organisations, and with the Central Bank. We met up with the team at World Education Cambodia and got them to explain our training approach and our educational methodologies. We also managed to fit in a visit to Siem Reap and Angkor Wat, where we all got up early one morning to watch the sun rise behind the ancient temple.

Almost all of the board members had been to a developing country before, but mostly as tourists. Everyone was already very interested in our work and deeply committed, but there's nothing to beat the experience of going out to a poor, remote village and meeting the beneficiaries to reinforce that commitment. It was such a huge opportunity. Two of our board members had been on a trip to the Philippines that we'd organised the year before. It was a fundraising trip, a combination of adventure and education, and they'd climbed a mountain and stayed in villages. But this trip to Cambodia was different. It gave the board members the opportunity to talk directly to our beneficiaries about their work and their families, how they ran their savings groups, and how they managed loans.

One woman they met was running a small business raising broiler chickens. She'd needed to borrow $100 to get her broiler business started. She explained to the group how she'd borrowed the money through her savings group, and how she had learned – from the training we'd provided – about looking after her chickens, about keeping them healthy and feeding them the right kind of food. We explained to the board members that when a someone receives a loan to start a small business, like this woman's broiler chicken business, we provide them with the training they need to run the business successfully. That's not just technical training, it's also financial training. Talking to that woman, they heard how much she'd paid for each chicken and how much she could sell them for; how she'd paid off her loan and put a little of her profit aside to buy the next batch of chickens.

And then, while the group were talking to the woman, a girl of about eight or nine joined them.

The woman introduced her to the group. 'This is my daughter,' she said. 'She's now going to school. That uniform she's wearing: I bought that uniform with the money I made selling my chickens. I learned how to run my business profitably from the training that you gave me.'

Listening to that woman, and hearing the pride in her voice as she told her story, made everyone smile. They got it. They understood in a way that was real – much more real than reading a report on how savings and loans programs work. What we're doing genuinely makes a difference to people's lives. Some of the board members hadn't fully understood how our microfinance programs work; others understood how the programs work in theory, but not in practice. Talking to that woman, and others like her, the board members saw for themselves how the programs work on the ground. It made the world of a difference. They came away from that trip really understanding how savings and loans can transform people's lives. It closed the circle wonderfully.

Of course, the stories we heard weren't all successful. We talked to a few people who'd taken out loans to set up a small business – chickens, goat rearing, vegetable growing – and the chickens had died or the crops had failed, and they'd lost the money. This is why savings are so important. Savings must come first. The problem with savings is that it doesn't work as a fundraiser. You can't engage with the Australian public around the idea of savings; they're not going to donate to support savings programs. So we promote the lending side of our work. People don't realise that we focus more on savings and education, and that the loans side of what we do accounts for only a small part of our work and our income.

One approach that Good Return has taken that's been really successful is to introduce a system for our lenders to make regular loans, where they can set up a debit order. In other words, you can set and forget $30 a month. You can also set it up so that your loans automatically become donations. It's taken the last two or three years to get this in place: the cost of technology is very high. Setting up a system for regular donations is really easy. Setting up a system for loans, on the other hand, is really complicated. It's complicated because the loans are provided in different currencies. The repayments every month then have to be tracked in various currency exchange rates, and then reconciled and sent back to the lender. We could lend the money in Australian dollars, but we deliberately made the decision to provide loans in the local currency. The women we are working with, who we're lending to, can't afford the risk of borrowing in Aussie dollars, with variable exchange rates. It wouldn't be fair to them: they're living on the equivalent of $2 or $3 a day. The organisation that's working with them doesn't want to take the risk either, whereas the Australian who's lending $100 can easily take a $5 hit – or possibly make a gain, as the case might be.

Lending in local currencies is one of the things that differentiates Good Return from Kiva, the US non-profit online lending program. They're much bigger than us, and very strong technically, but they only process loans in US dollars. Our approach means that we are more accessible to people in countries like Cambodia, Nepal and the Philippines who need the loans. And we are the only NGO in Australia – in fact, in the whole of Asia – to run an online lending program.

∞

In banking jargon, we're not actually providing loans; we're providing surety for loans. We provide capital to our partners, the local microfinance institutions – an NGO, perhaps, or a credit union – in the form of interest-free loans. Because that money is interest-free, the institutions aren't paying for that capital. That means they can charge a lower interest rate to their clients, and that means they can lend to more people. So the money we provide to the local partner, the microfinance institution, benefits that organisation and all their clients.

It's hard explaining to people that their money doesn't go directly to the individual that they've chosen to lend to. One person once asked me, 'I sent my money to Rose on Monday. Has she received it yet?' They didn't understand that their donation, together with many other people's donations, are part of the income we generate to distribute to our partner organisations in Cambodia, in Fiji, in Nepal, in the Philippines and all the other countries where we're working. Of course, Rose will receive her loan, but it's through the local partner organisation, a microfinance institution such as an NGO or a credit union, that her savings group works with. She probably doesn't know much about Good Return. The partner organisation may have talked to her group about Good Return, but that won't mean much to Rose. All she knows is that the money she borrows from the partner organisation partly comes from Australia. The organisation will have explained to her and the others in her group that the money they borrow is from donations made by the public online. They'll have explained that they need to take the women's photographs to put up on the internet, so that members of the public will see who they're lending to. Rose will need to give her permission for her picture to be taken, and she'll know it's to encourage Australians to donate money. But the important thing is not whether Rose knows about Good Return or where her money will come from. What's important is that she will receive her loan, and the interest she pays on that loan is reduced because we've provided the capital to the microfinance institution at zero interest. That means all of the members of Rose's group benefit. They are all able to access low-interest loans. That's the important point.

Most people – even very poor people – can usually find ways to borrow money, especially if they're desperate. But borrowing from a local moneylender, for example, will cost them an exorbitant amount in interest. In the Philippines, for example, they have this 'five-sixths' system of lending: you borrow 50 pesos, say, and at the end of the week you pay back 60 pesos. That's twenty per cent a week. Over a year, twenty per cent compounded over fifty-two weeks – that's over ten thousand per cent!

The equivalent in Australia, I guess, are payday lenders – people who lend money at exorbitant rates for very short terms, to be repaid when the borrower next gets paid. The government is forever trying to control payday lenders and reduce the interest rates they charge and force them out of business. The reason they exist, of course, is that there's a gap in the market. It's the same in the countries where we're working. People are paying these huge rates because they have no choice. They're not stupid; they know that they are paying too much interest. They may not be able to calculate exactly how much, but they know they're paying a lot. And they'd much rather be paying eighteen per cent a year than ten thousand per cent, or whatever it is.

The fact is that there isn't enough capital for microfinance institutions to provide loans to everyone. But with the money that Good Return is able to lend them, interest free, they can give out thousands more loans every year. By providing microfinance institutions with capital, we're not only helping the poor; we're also helping the institutions themselves. On the strength of the capital we lend them, they can then increase their borrowings from other sources, which means they can benefit more poor people. It's like the equity you have in your house: the more equity you have, the less interest you'll have to pay on your mortgage, so your equity is actually worth more than its initial dollar value. It's the same with the interest-free capital that we provide to the microfinance institutions: it's worth a lot more than the amount we actually give them. That's great; that's how we can make a real difference.

An important focus of our work has been around building the capacity of the microfinance institutions, as well as the capacity of our clients. Our method has been to train trainers to train others, either community trainers or trainers within the microfinance institution. We work on improving their financial systems, their management systems, their risk management systems, and detailed work related to skills development, like preparing training materials on how to manage savings and loans.

One of the things that's really good about building the capacity of our partner organisations and financial institutions is that we're effectively putting in place an exit strategy from the very start. Right from when we begin providing support to our partners, we start planning around how we're going to reduce and eventually withdraw that support. We'll often have an exit strategy of three to five years. Sometimes we stay with an organisation up to seven years. The aim is to ensure that an organisation is financially sustainable and has sound governance and management systems. By building their capacity both financially and in terms of skills and systems, we're able to withdraw support and move on to help someone else. So our work isn't only about microfinance; it's not only about helping the individual. Good Return is helping literally hundreds of thousands of people by helping financial institutions to operate sustainably on their own.

∞

It was at the development bank in Uganda that I gained practical experience in delivering programs. I was an implementer. I learned about the day-to-day work, the technical skills and methods around training. Then later, as a consultant, I learned about the theory of training methodologies: I read books, I did that course on microfinance at the University of Colorado in the US. But there's nothing like being responsible for an organisation's strategy and having to make decisions around how to implement that strategy to force you to be clear in your thinking about why microfinance is so important. I've heard people say, 'Why don't you do more loans?' Well, provided you have the funds, giving someone a loan is easy; getting it repaid is difficult. How you manage the risks, and how you provide the loans at low cost: I learned those things early on. It was the rationale around why we do these things, not just how we do them, that I learned at FINCA, and from FINCA onwards.

But even working for a microfinance organisation like FINCA didn't give me the depth of knowledge that I was hoping for. That's what drove me to set up my own organisation: the desire to make my own decisions and apply what I'd learned at FINCA and at the microfinance course in Colorado in ways that I believed would have the most impact. To take that knowledge to the next step. Ultimately this is what drove me to set up an NGO, rather than a consultancy: wanting to make a difference to the lives of hundreds of thousands of people. Perhaps, unconsciously, it was an attempt to compensate for the guilt I felt about not staying in South Africa to make a difference there.

For me, an NGO, or a community-based organisation, or a charity – whatever you want to call it – is a values-based organisation. That means a commitment to authenticity, inclusivity, mutual respect – those kinds of values. I've always been conscious of wanting to establish a culture of transparency, of openness, of respect for each other: an egalitarian culture. These values permeate the culture of the organisation. Our values are our culture. Whether someone is joining the organisation as a board member, or as part of the management team, or as a volunteer, I want to make them feel part of the community of Good Return. I sit them down for an hour and get to know them. I tell them about why I started Good Return and what the organisation aspires to achieve. A lot of people who have come to work with us have told me they feel a unique sense of belonging, of being part of something special. Take the example of our volunteers: we have hundreds of volunteers, and they are made to feel like they are a part of the team; they're no different from the paid staff members. They're treated with the same respect; they're given the same opportunities to take part in trainings and fundraising events. That increases their buy-in and their commitment. That's why most of them never leave. They're part of the family.

For years, I've resisted having an organisational chart. I didn't want to represent Good Return in the conventional way, as a triangle, with me at the top and most of the staff at the bottom. As CEO, you have certain rights, of course: rights and responsibilities. Everyone knows you have those rights. You don't have to force them down people's throats.

∞

Over the years, there have been a lot of changes in Good Return. We have learned from experience, and we have evolved. One of the biggest changes in recent years is that local people in the countries where we work have started to provide some of the services that we were providing in the early years, and they're providing those services more cheaply and perhaps better than we are able to. Technical specialists, IT people, accountants, management consultants – those sorts of people. In our work in Nepal, for example, there's been a cadre of accountants that have developed over the last couple of decades who are now able to provide accountancy services to our microfinance partners in Nepal. We would've provided those services in the past. Similarly, IT consultants have started being able to provide the IT support to our partners in Asia in the last five years or so which we provided previously. So, in response to these changes, we've become a more specialised agency.

The second big change in the way Good Return works is that we focus much more now on consumer protection. This shift is a direct result of growth in the microfinance sector. Our programs have grown.

We are reaching more and more people, and increasing numbers of people are able to access loans. And that's a good thing, as long as there are proper rules in place, and as long as the microfinance services are being done in such a way as to reduce the risks of over-indebtedness. But even with these safeguards in place, the fact is that debt can be a heavy burden to a poor person. It's troubled me, the possibility that we could be putting people into debt that they can't afford. As a consequence, we have focused very heavily on consumer protection, ensuring that we're protecting the poor and vulnerable. We're doing a lot of work with central banks and the governments of countries like Cambodia and Vietnam. It's not just about keeping interest rates low, although of course that's important too. It's about financial education. I still use the old-fashioned term 'financial literacy'. But in fact it's not simply financial literacy, it's capability: giving people the knowledge to understand what kinds of things they should use loans for and what a loan will actually cost them. Understanding the risks of taking a loan and understanding that they have the right to turn down a loan. In other words, empowering them.

We've also changed the way we evaluate our training courses and how we measure success. In the development sector, when you evaluate a training activity to see how successful it's been, there's a tendency to measure outputs: how many courses you've delivered, how many people you've trained, and so on. There's been less of a focus on the outcomes of that training. There's an important difference between outputs and outcomes. Take the example of running a carpentry course: you train ten people to be carpenters, and at the end of the training they're able to make a table the way they've been taught. That's the output: ten people have been trained. You go back six months later and you look at whether or not they're still applying those carpentry skills. You find that they're all still making tables the way they were taught; in other words, there's been a sustainable change in their behaviour as a result of their training. And that's the outcome. That's what you need to look for in development. That's what you measure as success.

So now we look at what people are doing six months or a year after the end of their training. If they're not using the skills we taught them, then there's probably something wrong with the way they've been taught. And that's led to changes in the way we deliver our training courses, tailoring our methods to suit people's needs and level of education, and getting them to repeat learned tasks and activities so that they internalise that knowledge and apply those skills appropriately. Ultimately, it's about empowerment. That's where consumer protection comes from: it's from people having the knowledge and power and skills and ability to form their own views and make their own decisions, to understand what's in their own interests and to make those interests known. The most powerful thing is knowledge; knowledge is power.

∞

The three biggest challenges we face as a planet, I believe, are climate change, poverty and global inequality. I can't do much about number one and number three, other than make regular donations to Greenpeace, but I've spent years trying to help eradicate poverty. I'm also involved in a program at Macquarie University, teaching in what's called the Global Leadership Program. The program is about identifying the big issues that will face future leaders and policy makers: issues around ethics, poverty, and climate change. What I'm trying to do is alert the new generation to these issues. I'm trying to help them understand that our response to these issues is about making choices, and that the choices that leaders make have to be justified. You have to understand the reasons why you make certain choices. The reasons for eradicating poverty, for example, may be economic, security-related or ethical – or a combination of all three.

I try to get the students to understand firstly that global poverty is one of the biggest challenges facing us. It's closely linked to inequality. I make the point that inequality is not sustainable; it's not sustainable between communities, within communities, across regions, within countries. I explain that poverty has direct links with international security. Poverty and inequality breed discontent, and discontent breeds social upheaval. At its most extreme, it finds expression in terrorism. There's the economic argument and the security argument; then I put forward the moral argument for why we should tackle poverty.

Mostly I talk to the students about the ethics of poverty and inequality. I point out to them that trying to overcome inequality and poverty for purely ethical reasons has merit in itself. I use the example given by Peter Singer, the Australian philosopher based at Princeton.

His example goes something like this. You're going for a walk and you come to a pond. There's a young child in the water and he's obviously in trouble. If you don't do something fast, you know he's going to drown. They say that a drowning person comes up three times before they go down forever. This kid has gone down a couple of times, and up again a couple of times. You're on the edge of this pond and you've got to act fast. The problem is, you're wearing a brand-new pair of $300 shoes. You realise you haven't got time to take your shoes off if you're going to jump in and save the kid. So what do you do? Do you jump in and ruin your shoes to save the child?

Well, of course you do! No one would say no. None of my students has ever said no. They're outraged at the suggestion! 'Of course we'd jump in!' they say. 'We wouldn't even think about it! $300 shoes? What's that in comparison with a child's life?'

And then I ask a question. 'Well, $300 is actually more than is needed to save the lives of the five thousand children who die every day from completely preventable diseases. So why aren't you giving those kids the $300 that would save their lives?'

I'm just trying to make a point; to get them to understand the ethical argument, the moral perspective.

Next, I talk to them about funding – how we can find the resources to invest in overcoming poverty. I give the example of funding for education. Education is one of the keys to solving problems of poverty and inequality, but even the Gates Foundation hasn't got enough money

*Good Return Sun Run fundraiser, from Dee Why to Manly, Sydney, 31 January 2015.*

to educate all the kids in the world. Then I launch into microfinance, and how it can go to scale. I explain that's one of its major strengths. If we have any hope of solving the world's problems, we need options that can go to scale. Microfinance is one of those options.

∞

After I received the news that my cancer had metastasised, I sat down with Neild Macintosh, who was chair of our board at that time, and I told him I thought I should step down as CEO.

'Let's just see how it goes,' he said. 'Give it a bit of time.'

That seemed fair. But given my prognosis, I assured him I'd make a decision before the end of 2015.

Not long after that, on 31 January 2015, about seventy Good Return staff, volunteers, board members and supporters took part in a fundraising Sun Run organised by the *Sydney Morning Herald*. I had bet one of our ambassadors, the paralympian gold medallist Heath Francis, which one of us would finish first. He gave me an hour handicap and still won! I certainly wasn't fit enough to run, so I walked the whole distance – just under seven kilometres – from Dee Why to Manly. The fun run was a huge success: not only did we get some great publicity, but we also we raised a significant amount of donations. I raised over $6,000 myself from friends, family and connections. I may not have been able to beat Heath to the finishing line, but I managed to beat him in donations! In terms of my health, however, my participation came at a heavy cost: I was left completely exhausted. For the next four days, I was hardly able to leave my bed.

Towards the end of that year, I informed the Good Return board that I was going to resign and that we needed to start looking for a replacement. Because it was close to Christmas, I waited until after the holidays to tell the staff and everyone else that I was stepping down as CEO.

It took from January till about July before we finally appointed the new CEO. Our new chair, Kate Jordan, led the recruitment with an executive employment agency. I thought – and the board strongly supported the idea – that inviting applicants from outside Good Return was good practice. We also hoped there'd be internal applicants – and there were. One of these was Shane. In the end, it came down to Shane as the internal candidate, and an excellent external candidate. Ultimately, the board felt that Shane was the strongest choice: he had helped to found the organisation and get it off the ground. Appointing him as CEO ensured the organisational culture and institutional memory of Good Return would be maintained.

I thought it would be difficult, stepping down as CEO. I thought it would be hard to let go. I thought that I'd be anxious about handing over the reins. In fact, the opposite was true. My last day as CEO was 31 August 2016, and six days later I turned fifty-five. As a young uni student, I thought success was retiring at fifty-five! My thoughts on that certainly changed over the years, but I did retire at fifty-five. And all I felt was relief. Partly it was my health, and partly it was that handing over to Shane felt natural. I felt comfortable. Shane had demonstrated over many years that he had great value and a commitment to our mission and our vision. He'd helped to shape these things, of course.

It was a relief to know that I could let go. I knew that I hadn't been working at a hundred per cent for the previous couple of months before retiring. I was doing forty hours a week – but that was well below what I had been doing previously. For many years, I'd worked fifty-five to sixty hours a week. When I travelled, I'd often fly out on a Sunday and fly back on a Saturday. I gave up a lot of time with the family for Good Return.

On reflection, I think that you can be CEO for too long. I had my eye taken out almost exactly ten years after I started World Education Australia, and I stayed on as CEO for another three years after that. Perhaps I should've handed the reins over to Shane when I lost my eye. Ten years as CEO is probably long enough. As the leader, you need to bring new ideas, new energy, new strategies, new ways of thinking to the organisation. And I was probably running out of ideas, running out of energy. What did Einstein say? The definition of insanity is doing the same thing repeatedly and expecting a different result! To grow, to improve and achieve different results – better results – you need to experiment, you need to take risks. That takes energy. That takes a new leader. Now, although Shane had been in the organisation almost from the start, I had definitely been the leader. He's said that it's only now, since taking on the CEO role, that he's realised how the buck stops with him. Previously it was always me. He would come up with an idea, but ultimately I was the one who had to make the decision. Now he has to carry the can and worry about making payroll every month. It's his responsibility.

In the early days, I confess I had to borrow money out of our home loan occasionally to make payroll. Jacqui agreed, but of course she was worried about whether we'd get the money back. Fair enough! There were times when I wasn't sure when we'd get it back, to be honest; we'd often be waiting for months to be paid by the government or by one of the international development agencies. So I borrowed the money to keep the cash flow going. It was a bit of a risk, of course, certainly in the early days. We probably had half a dozen staff at that time. I certainly didn't tell them at the time that I was borrowing money out of my own home loan to make payroll. It wouldn't have filled them with confidence – they might have started looking for other jobs! But you've got to do whatever it takes to make sure that the business is a success. I don't think that it's good business practice, necessarily, but I guess it's a reflection of my commitment to the organisation and the sacrifices that we as a family have made. And it's one aspect of the responsibility you have as CEO to make payroll every month – a responsibility that Shane has definitely felt since taking over the role. Whether you're the CEO of an organisation with five staff or a thousand staff, you have a responsibility to your staff and to the team. You've got to pay them first, before you do anything else. You pay your staff before you pay your suppliers. Not that suppliers aren't critical, but you've got to look after the family first, if you like.

I'm sure it would be different if I was working in the commercial sector and selling investments and widgets to institutional investors. I don't know that I would bring my work home in the same way. I'm not saying that Good Return is a family business – we have independent directors and so on – but the boundaries between my working life and my family have always been blurred. I've often had work colleagues, staff and board members stay at our house, and we've held our staff Christmas parties at home. I talk about Good Return to anyone and everyone we meet. The kids tease me about that: 'Oh, Dad, please don't talk about Good Return to the waiter!' On the one hand, they're really proud of Good Return, and of what I do; on the other hand, it's a case of 'Oh no! – Dad's on this mission again!', and they groan and roll their eyes, the way kids do.

Since stepping down as CEO, I've cut back a bit. One of my New Year's resolutions at the end of 2017 was to reconsider how much work I do. I was on four boards at that time: the Salvation Army's international development board; the Good Return board; Habitat for Humanity Australia; and I had recently joined the board of SEEP (Small Enterprise and Education Program) as a director. In the English-speaking world, SEEP is the premier non-profit small enterprise and microfinance association. They've got about ninety-six members across eighty countries. At the beginning of 2018, I made the decision to resign from the Salvation Army board to cut back on my workload.

My work for each of the boards takes up about one day a month, so that's one day a week, on average. I still work at Good Return a few days a week, when I'm well enough. I spend another forty hours a year teaching and preparation, so that's another five days a year, or half a day a month. I actually spend more time at the doctors now than I do on my teaching or board work. I suppose I spend about one day a fortnight on medical stuff, one way or another. Sometimes it's more, like when I have radiation treatment, but it's been something along those lines. Then there have been the emergency visits to the hospital, and the side effects...

One of the things that I've been reflecting on recently is why I started Good Return. Some people have suggested to me that it's because I'm religious, or spiritual. There were many factors, but being religious wasn't one of them. I was playing squash one day with a friend, and after the game we got chatting about the work that we did. Another guy overheard us, and as he left the changing room he put his head back around the corner and said to me, 'God bless you. You're a good Christian.' I'm not a good Christian. I'm not an engaged Christian. I don't go to church. I think that I have a relationship with God, but is it a Christian God? I don't know. I do believe in the traditional Christian values – honesty, kindness, tolerance, charity, that kind of thing. I was brought up with those values, especially around helping others: the story of the good Samaritan. I try to live by those values.

I read an article recently in the *Sydney Morning Herald* about people who have been told that they have terminal cancer. When they look back on their life, what are their regrets? Interestingly, few people had regrets about the things that they had done. Most people had regrets about the things they hadn't done. I always wanted to take risks, make things happen. That was a large part of what drove me to start Good

Return. And coupled with this, my views on humanity and Christian values.

I've had many people say to me, 'You're doing such good work – I wish I could do that too.'

I say to those people, 'Well, why don't you? It's your choice.'

They say, 'Oh, I can't – there's the family, the mortgage – I can't take the risk.'

But that's still a choice. Like Jean Paul Sartre said, you can always choose; but if you choose not to choose, you should recognise that that's still a choice. Life is about making choices. I've chosen to do certain things, and that means I've chosen not to do something else. I chose to start an NGO. I still had to earn money; I still had a family to support, a mortgage to pay. Other people could have made the same choice if they'd wanted to.

So, if someone says to me, 'I wish I could do what you've done', and if they're really serious about it, I'd like to say to them, 'Follow what David Livingstone, the explorer, once said: "Sympathy is no substitute for action."'

## 11

# Facing the bully

'The truth is a bully we all pretend to like' – Gregory David Roberts

Guy describes himself as being in denial, but I'm not convinced. Perhaps he was in denial initially, when he first got the diagnosis that his cancer was terminal:

'When the cancer metastasised,' he says, 'first in my liver and then in my bones, I didn't want to tell everyone. It would make it too real.'

That was just in the first few months after the diagnosis. But now, when he talks about the disease – its treatment, the side effects, and the way it impacts on his life, every day – he is utterly straightforward. His own mortality is a theme he keeps going back to, tentatively exploring what it might mean. The truth may be a bully, but Guy has faced the bully, and his response is simply to get on with life.

Early on he told me, 'What's the point of sitting in a corner being miserable for whatever time you've got left?'

Indeed. He has his low moments, of course. But Guy is definitely not a man to be bullied.

Today, he tells me the story from the beginning.

∞

The memory of that night when the melanoma was discovered in my eye has taken on that hyper-real quality that comes with the most extreme moments of trauma. It's similar, in a way, to my memory of that moment as a conscript in Angola, when the shell I'd fired exploded against a tree and the truth dawned on me that I would've died had the explosive not been accidentally replaced by a smoke bomb. Except in this case, the discovery of the melanoma felt like the explosive was real. No smoke bomb this time.

For a few days, I had been experiencing a strange haziness in my left eye. I kept thinking it would simply go away, but I finally left work early and went to see my GP. I expected to be prescribed some eye drops and that would be the end of it. It was a shock to hear that he thought my retina was detaching and that I needed to go straight to emergency at the Sydney Eye Hospital. He stressed that it wasn't safe for me to drive myself there. I rushed back to tell Jacqui, who was in bed with a black eye and a broken arm following a cycling accident a few days before. She also couldn't drive, so David, her father, came to the rescue and drove us through the dusk to the eye hospital. In the meantime, Jacqui searched online for information about detached retinas. What she'd found was pretty alarming: sometimes the damage can be permanent and your sight never recovers. The treatment involved immediate surgery and several days' complete bed rest.

We arrived at Sydney Eye Hospital as night was falling. We found our way through the hospital complex of beautiful old sandstone buildings to the emergency department and took a seat in the waiting room. After about twenty minutes a young resident called us through and examined my eye. He looked into it for a long time. Then, with hardly a word, he left the room and returned a minute or two later with his supervisor. Once again, there was a long examination of my eye. I'm pretty squeamish and have never liked anyone touching my eyes, but I wasn't especially worried at that stage. The two doctors then left the room to confer, and when they came back in they said that they had asked the consultant to drive in from his home to see me. I began to feel uneasy.

It was about nine o'clock that night when the consultant arrived. He examined my eye and then broke the news very directly. 'Mr Winship, I'm afraid you have a large tumour behind your left eye. The tumour mass is as a result of ocular melanoma.'

I was stunned. I'd never even heard of a melanoma occurring in the eye. A detached retina suddenly seemed trivial.

Jacqui pressed him for more details. 'What does this mean? How bad is it?'

'Mrs Winship,' he replied, 'if a melanoma of this size were on your husband's skin, he would already be dead. As it is, the best case scenario is that he will only lose his eye.'

There was silence in the car as David drove us home. We were all in shock. When we got home, Jacqui and I went up to bed. We lay awake in the dark, holding hands. It felt like this was a bad dream that we would wake up from in the morning.

The next day, after a sleepless night, my first instinct was not to tell anyone. I guess I hoped that the specialist would tell us that it was all a mistake. But Jacqui persuaded me that we needed to deal with this the way we did all things – with the support of our family and friends. As soon as the kids left for school – still largely unaware of what was happening – we drove to the home of our very good friends, Brett and Rose-Anne Hawkeswood. We shared the news, hugged, wept and began calling other close friends and family members. A small group soon gathered at the Hawkeswoods – old friends from Durban days. One dear friend, Lyndsay Brown, began doing some research for us. Usually this is Jacqui's role, and later she would become an expert on ocular melanoma, but at that point she was too shocked and frightened to read anything. Lyndsay reassured us slightly by telling us that although there was a fifty per cent chance of the cancer spreading, there was an equal chance that it might not. Suddenly I was eager to have my eye removed – to get rid of the cancer and get on with life.

Having your eye removed is traumatic. The surgery is performed under local anaesthetic, so you're aware of everything that's happening. But I recovered quickly; the worst of the pain was over in about five days, and the news was good: the margins were clear. I would need annual scans to check for metastatic spread, but that was fine. Ever the optimist, I pushed the risk out of my mind and got back to business as usual. I soon adjusted to seeing the world through one eye.

The year flew by, and when I went in for my scan in November

*Guy with Good Return staff celebrating International Day of the Girl,
11 October 2013, a fortnight after Guy had his left eye surgically removed.
L to R: Sandra Carvajal, Jessie Fisher, Lesley Hume, Guy, Sujinda Hwang-Leslie,
Joni Freeman, Loma Asker, Norm Sturrock, Sarah Webster, Michael Walker.*

2014, I felt pretty confident. But later that day Jacqui phoned me in tears. She had picked up the radiology report from the hospital and read the results. They showed several suspicious growths in my liver.

My oncologist, Alex Guminski, didn't tell me straight away how long I'd got. He sent a message to say that he needed to see me to discuss the results, so I booked the earliest available appointment. Jacqui and I went to see him together. She had done a lot of research by that stage and knew what might be coming. She was so anxious that she kept having to run to the toilet. I was worried too, of course, but I wasn't as well informed as she was.

A few minutes into the appointment, Alex broke the news that the cancer had metastasised.

I gripped Jacqui's hand. 'So…what's the treatment?' I asked.

'I'm sorry, Guy,' Alex said. 'There isn't a cure.'

'What do you mean there isn't a cure?' I asked, not quite comprehending.

'It's terminal, I'm afraid,' Alex answered.

'So…are you saying I need to start getting my affairs in order?'

'Yes, that would be wise.'

For a few moments, no one said anything. I felt utterly stunned, disbelieving. Beside me, I could hear Jacqui weeping quietly.

'So…how long?' It felt as though I was asking about someone else.

'Hard to say. A year…maybe longer.'

I remember walking up and down outside the corridor outside Alex's consulting rooms and thinking, this is completely surreal. I was fifty-three years old. I had a son, Thomas, who was fifteen, and a daughter, Brontë, who was eleven. I had a loving and healthy relationship. Life was good. I was running my own charity. I was financially secure. A lot of the hard work, the struggle of getting the charity going, had been done. But there was still a lot more I needed to do. A lot more I wanted to do. I wasn't young any more, but I certainly wasn't old.

We are all mortal. We just don't have to face up to it until we get told we've got a terminal disease. That is incredibly confronting. What do they say? – there are five or six different phases one goes through in grief: shock, disbelief, terror… I can't remember them all. Denial: this couldn't be happening to you. It's not real. Then not wanting to tell anyone, because telling people would make it real. Anger, disappointment. Then, gradually, understanding and acceptance, including reflecting on where you are in life and what you've done. Who you are as a person, what you wanted to achieve. Your relationship with others. Your place on this earth. Your own insignificance…

A few people have asked me, 'Now that this has happened to you, what's the great lesson?'

Truth is, I don't know if there is any great lesson. Just appreciate the ordinary things. Like early in the morning, I get up before Jacqui and the kids, and I go outside to the front of the house to get the newspaper. I walk to the end of the driveway, pick up the paper and look up at the sky. I appreciate whether it's a beautiful clear day at six in the morning, or whether it's raining; whether it's dark or light. I get this rush of appreciation for simple things. This might be my last day. That's perhaps the only lesson that I've learned.

∞

I remember the first Christmas after my cancer metastasised. Ever since we moved to Australia in 2002, we've had a big party on Christmas Eve – a gathering of what we call 'The Scatterlings of Africa', which is the title of a song by the famous South African band Juluka. We invite all our South African friends who are living here, many of whom don't have any family in Australia, to join us. Over the years, the gathering has grown to include a number of our Australian friends as well – honorary Scatterlings! – and with over forty guests, we serve a buffet-style dinner, with everyone bringing a dish to share. We usually hire a musician to play out on our deck in the early part of the evening and then gather around Joliette at the piano to sing carols. Later in the evening, things can get pretty raucous, with people dancing on tables and jumping fully clothed into our spa!

But the party on Christmas Eve 2014 was different. We'd only got the news about my prognosis a few weeks earlier and it still felt very raw. Without saying as much, Jacqui and I wondered whether this would be the last Christmas we'd have together. I could see that she was trying hard to make this Christmas a special one, but I wasn't feeling well as I had just started on treatment. I think everyone felt the weight of my diagnosis.

∞

In 2015, Jacqui and I went to stay for a week at the Gawler Foundation in Victoria. It was there that I learned mindfulness meditation, and I got into a routine of meditating regularly after that. In my little study upstairs, Brontë put together a little tray for me, with little stones on it. Each stone has a different word written on it: words like love, peace, trust, hope. I've got some incense and a candle; I used to light the candle and sit down and close my eyes. I kept up that routine for months, but I haven't been able to concentrate since going onto this treatment – particularly with the rash. I haven't done any meditation

*Guy's daughter, Brontë, with April, Sydney, 2016.*

for the last five or six months. My friend Gordon Cairns has been telling me to get back into it. He says I set the bar too high when I try to meditate for half an hour every day; a few minutes is enough. What he does, he says, when he's waiting for a meeting to start, or when he's in a doctor's waiting room, is he closes his eyes and he just meditates for five minutes. He says those five minutes are important. When all's said and done, it's about what works for you.

The sort of mindfulness training that I learned at the Gawler Foundation, that works for me. Jacqui and I learned to meditate together. Since then, I've meditated on my own. I've always felt that meditation was a solitary activity, I guess.

An old friend of mine in South Africa, Stephen Matthews, practises Sahaja meditation, and he's been encouraging me to join a group to do meditation here in Sydney. I guess if I can't concentrate enough to meditate on my own here at home, then doing it in a group with other people would be better than not doing it at all.

∞

## March 2017

Every two months, I get a CT scan. I have sleepless nights leading up to it. The scan results show how long I've got. Six months. Twelve months. Maybe longer. People say to me, 'You're going for another scan? How terrible!' But of course it's not the scan itself that's a worry. It's the results. That's what wakes me up at three o'clock in the morning.

It's the same routine each time: changing into the crisp cotton gown and waiting in the little cubicle outside where the CT scanner is. Then going in, lying down, feeling the needle going in, hearing the hum of the magnets going round and round. Getting the contrast put in and the brief sense of nausea in the back of your throat and the warmth in your pelvic area. You can feel a bit claustrophobic inside that machine. I know some people do. I don't, particularly. I've had MRIs, PET scans, and CT scans, so I'm kind of used to them. Going in every two months and following this routine, and then the next day, going to the oncologist with Jacqui and hearing the results: it's like going to meet the executioner. Finding out how long you have now. People all want certainty, but living with uncertainty is what you have to learn to do.

Initially, when I was told I had a year, the oncologist was exaggerating, because with this type of cancer, once it metastasises, in general you've only got six to nine months. So I've outlived that prognosis already, significantly. I'm well past my sell-by date! Of course, the bell curve takes into account everyone who gets diagnosed, and some people get diagnosed early, and some get diagnosed later, so it's just an estimate. An educated guess. Those who survive past the average are now living longer. We know of one woman with the same type of ocular cancer as me who has lasted fourteen years. She has a glass of wine every night! So...who knows?

The results from the latest scan revealed that a few of the tumours in my liver have grown a little, but for the moment this clinical trial I'm on seems to be keeping things reasonably stable, touch wood. I've been on the trial since November last year. It's testing an entirely new form of treatment that has been developed specifically for my type of metastasised ocular melanoma. The way it works is that it tries to cut off the tail-end of the protein molecule to inhibit the growth of the tumours.

The treatment comes with a bunch of side effects, of course. They say the side effects mean the drug is working. One side effect has been low blood pressure. I started on 1,000 milligrams a day and I collapsed when I had the first dose. I was one of two people in the world on that dosage trial: me and a woman in Holland. Both of us collapsed. They halved the dose to 500 milligrams, and then I developed this rash all over my body which I'm still trying to live with. They reduced the dose further. I still had the rash, so they reduced it to 300 milligrams. I'm still on 300 and I'm still battling with the rash. It got so bad a couple of months ago that I came off the treatment for about five days. So the drugs have side effects, but they're keeping me alive.

They're like cockroaches under the house, these tumours growing in your body. You can't see them, but you know they're there. Horrible, ugly things. You don't feel them in the liver, but you feel them in the bones; they tend to grow in the joint areas. The worst was in my right hip. That was painful all the time. Walking was hard. I had radiation for that in September last year. I didn't have any pain for about three months after that, but then the tumours came back. Two tumours grew in my side and broke three ribs. I was just starting this new treatment at the time and the oncologist said, 'Let's see if the treatment helps this.' In fact, it has reduced the tumours there. The ribs have healed; I don't get a lot of pain there now.

I've often said, and it's true: a day without pain is a good day. That's true for all of us. Having tumours all over your body brings your benchmark down a bit. Your standards for a good day come down somewhat. Being without pain is good. I'm having quite a few painless days with this treatment – and that's fantastic!

I don't know if it's good or bad, but I believe in suffering in silence. I don't believe that a pain shared is a pain halved; telling Jacqui just worries her and the family. Being stoic isn't for everyone, but one of the ways I deal with unhappiness is denial. It's a well-known psychological strategy – deny, deny, deny! I think dwelling on your pain, your suffering, your prognosis – I don't think it's healthy. Well, I don't know if it's healthy or not, but for me it doesn't contribute to anything.

There's so much that I still want to do. I'd love to be around to see Brontë finish high school in four years. She's in Year 8 now, so if I could see her finish high school, that would be fantastic. Thomas wants to do medicine, but I doubt that I'll ever see him become a doctor. Jacqui doesn't want to talk about what she will do. Will she have another relationship? She doesn't want to contemplate that possibility now. She doesn't want to talk about it.

Before I got this diagnosis, I used to tell a joke about a man asking his wife, 'What would you do if I got a terminal illness? Would you ever get remarried?'

His wife says, 'No, no, of course not!'

'Would you let him use my lovely car?'

'No, definitely not.'

'Would you let him use my surfboard?'

'No! Definitely not!'

'Would you let him use my golf clubs?'

'No – he's left-handed!'

I don't tell that joke now. It's too real.

∞

## July 2017

Jacqui made contact with a couple through Facebook around the middle of 2016. The husband had the same disease as me. He'd lost an eye, and then the disease metastasised, just like mine. There aren't many people in Sydney with ocular melanoma: it's such a rare disease. Jacqui was keen to meet them, so we arranged to meet them for lunch.

One of the first signs that things weren't looking good for this guy was when his liver function went down a few weeks ago. My liver function was tested last week and it had also gone down. Not a good sign. Shortly afterwards, I saw my oncologist, who told me that the man had just died.

Three things – David's death last month, this other man's death soon after, and my liver function going down – truthfully, they've knocked me about. I've been lying awake at night, worrying about my mortality. I have a very good capacity to bounce back and I'm sure that I'll be fine. I'm not easily depressed. But this journey, if that's what it is, can sometimes seem a bit of a marathon. It's not like a stroke or a heart attack. You can't stay positive all the time.

The reason that I don't connect with other people with the disease, and haven't joined the Melanoma Institute, or cancer groups, or stayed in touch with people on the same trial as me, is because they keep dying. It's too confronting. It's also completely selfish of me, but I don't want to invest in a relationship that's not going to last. I don't have the time. That's being brutally honest.

Since David died in June, my view has shifted. I'm less sure now about whether being stoic is a good thing. He never complained, never expressed how he was feeling. I wonder now whether that stoicism was helpful – either to him or the family. I'm no longer so sure that not talking about one's problems is a good thing. I don't want to share more than I need to, but I don't any longer think that being stoic is always the best way. People who care about you want to hear about your pain, although even your most loved ones might not want to know about every intimate detail. I oscillate between wanting to be stoic and wanting to share. Sometimes denial is an effective way of dealing with something. Just putting it out of my mind. Trying not to think about the pain. Not dwelling in the unhappiness of the disease. Yeah…happiness is a decision.

∞

## 6 September 2017

Today Guy turns fifty-six. It's been a busy couple of weeks since we last spoke. His brother Jonathan and his wife Sue were visiting from England with their children, and they all spent a few days together in the Whitsundays.

A couple of days ago, Guy sent me a brief email: 'I'm back in Sydney – and raring to go!'

I was hesitant to arrange a phone call this morning, given that it was his birthday, but he was keen to go ahead.

Guy rings on the dot of nine. His voice on the phone is flat. He sounds tired, not his usual ebullient self. He has no interest in chatting about the holiday. He wants to get straight down to the business of recording this next conversation. But before he hits the record button, he tells me two things: first, he's bought a new car, an Audi convertible ('my birthday present to myself!' he says with a chuckle); and second, he had another scan last Monday.

The results show that my tumours have grown. A new tumour has appeared on one of my major organs. I'm also starting to get some pain. I haven't said anything to Jacqui and the kids, but I can definitely feel something. I definitely have some pain.

I'll have another scan at the end of the month to see if the tumours have grown again. Sometimes they grow and then stop growing for a while. If the next scan shows they've continued to grow, then well, I don't know. Maybe surgery is an option, or radiation... But there are complications...

∞

## Late September 2017

I've been waking up at night a lot. I have pretty severe chest pain from an infection in my lungs, and every time I turn over I wake up. Not only is the pain the problem, it's also the lack of sleep because I keep waking up and I can't get back to sleep. And when I do eventually get back to sleep, I turn over and then my ribs hurt and my chest hurts and so I wake up again. It's hard not to feel a bit maudlin at three o'clock in the morning. It's a low point in the night when you feel most vulnerable and least protected.

The association between pain and death is unavoidable. Pain brings the horizon closer, whereas the absence of pain pushes that horizon away. I've had quite a lot of pain in the last couple of weeks and that has been confrontational. Every breath hurts, and it makes me think maybe I've got pneumonia again, or the tumour in my side has broken a couple more ribs. It feels like that. That association with death has been a link that my cortex has just responded to in a primeval, primitive sort of way… It's just a cold, clingy, horrible feeling that that horizon is coming closer. But now, today, I woke up pain-free and sort of happy, and the horizon recedes again… As I always say, a day without pain is a good day.

Pain management isn't something I've looked at in detail. I guess I've tried to avoid thinking about it. My understanding is that pain is going to be part of the journey, and I am fearful of that. Pain is different from death, the idea of death. Death is an absence of something. You're either here or you're not here. But pain is real. Pain is immediate. Pain is confronting in a way that death isn't. Pain is much more engaging. It's very real. In pain, you know that you're here. You definitely know that you're alive.

Pain has become an old friend, if that makes sense. It's become a little familiar. It's like a backache, I guess. You wake up with backache and you know you're alive.

I don't like talking about death, but these last couple of weeks, when I was in hospital, I've had a lot of time to reflect on things. Jacqui came to see me every day, but apart from her and the kids, I didn't have any other visitors because the hospital is a bit out of town. I had a lot of time to reflect. I don't have any sense of what there is after death. I've thought about it long and hard and I don't have any sense of what's beyond the body. With David's death just a couple of months ago, when we were gathered around his body it didn't feel as if there was anything there. It felt like his soul, or his spirit, or however you term it, had left his body. It had gone. I don't know where it had gone, or if it simply remained in our memories; but there was definitely a sense of the absence of that spirit. It was just a body. But I have no sense of what's beyond that. I've looked for inspiration in those early hours, when I can't sleep, and I've got nothing. I don't know if other people see more.

Another thing that happened is that the pneumonia left me feeling drained. Not only physically drained, but emotionally washed out as well. That's the way I described it to Jacqui. Washed-out. Partly from the pain, and partly from the lack of sleep. It also made me think that there are going to be more episodes like this ahead, and that made me feel a little scared. The mouth of the tunnel yawned in front of me, in a way that it hadn't done before.

My mother used to say, 'Getting old isn't for sissies.' Not for the faint-hearted.

I can tell you that cancer is not for the faint-hearted, either.

## 12

## What is a good life?

*'There are only two ways to live your life: one is as though nothing is a miracle; the other is as though everything is a miracle'* – Flora Winship

Guy has lived his life with passion and indefatigable energy, driven by a determination to make a difference and change the world for the better. For Guy, life is about making choices, and many of those choices have been prompted by the idea of doing good: specifically, helping the poor to improve their lives. In our conversations he returned again and again to the idea of good: what it means to lead a good life, to be a good person, the desire to do good. The idea of a good God, guiding our choices. Good being the outcome of those choices – the acts of love, kindness, generosity. The Ugandan villager who saves every spare shilling from selling fabric in the market to send her daughter to high school. The schoolteacher who donates $50 of her modest salary every month to charity. The retired actuary who volunteers in a soup kitchen. The high-powered businessman who devotes a chunk of his limited free time to working for a charity. To Guy, these acts are the result of choices to do good, to give something back.

There was a study a few years ago on Australians' understanding of foreign aid: how much they believe Australia gives, and how much they think we should give. A lot of people said they thought Australia gives about ten per cent of its budget to foreign aid. When asked how much we should give, they responded that it shouldn't be more than five per cent.

One time I was visiting AusAID headquarters in Canberra, and I had just landed at Canberra Airport. I caught a taxi outside the terminal and asked the taxi driver to take me to AusAID.

The driver said, 'Oh, so you work in aid? Giving our money away!'

'That's right,' I said. 'How much money do you think it is?'

'Oh,' he said, 'it's billions!'

'Okay,' I said, 'how much, d'you think, as a percentage of the government's income?'

'I dunno,' he said. 'Maybe ten per cent.'

When I told him it's less than one per cent, and less than one quarter of one per cent of our country's income, he told me straight out that I was a liar.

This is one of the things that I say to conservative audiences: the amount we as a country spend on foreign aid is vastly less than most people think. The aid budget in 2017 was worth about $3.8 billion: far less than we spend on the refugee camps in Manus and Nauru. I heard in the news the other day that Australia has spent $10 billion on so-called detention centres. We could do so much good with that money. We could improve the lives of refugees in the camps in Pakistan, in Malaysia, in Thailand. We could do so much good there. That good work would earn Australia such a good name, and it wouldn't cost half as much as the bad work we do with the asylum seekers offshore. This argument isn't just about doing the right thing; it's about economics and rationalism. It's also about regional security. By locking people away, we're helping to radicalise them. Instead, if we were doing good work in refugee camps in Pakistan or Afghanistan, or in Iraq or in Turkey, we as a nation would look so much better. We would be de-radicalising, and it would cost us a lot less – let alone the good works that we would be seen to be doing and sharing our own values of fairness and equality and a fair go. We're a global community, with global responsibilities, quite apart from the moral imperative that we should share the wealth that we've had the good fortune to enjoy in Australia.

A couple of years ago, I read that Australia was the richest country in the world, per capita, of all countries with a population over ten million. Norway and Sweden, Switzerland, Monte Carlo and Luxembourg – small countries like that – all had higher per capita incomes, but they're tiny. With a population of over ten million, we were the richest country in the world. Hell, we can afford to help a little bit! Helping others is part of the dynamic in the global village, not only the local village. Think of someone in Australia giving a loan to someone in Nepal; that's an act of doing good in the global sense.

In terms of public donations, the Australian public is actually quite generous. I think we're in the top six countries in the world. But we are in the top one or two in terms of volunteering. When I think of all the volunteers who work for Good Return – professionals, highly skilled people, willing to give us their time and energy because they believe in what we do – it's really amazing. They give us one, two, or three days a week for years, working really hard. Some go overseas for months, or for a whole year, as field support officers. When we advertise for a volunteer to fill a position, say for someone with particular specialist skills, we often get thirty or forty people applying – many of them with top qualifications and years of professional experience. That's for an unpaid position! Our volunteers have really been the backbone of Good Return. We couldn't have done what we've done without them. We sometimes struggle for finances, but we always have people ready to put their shoulder to the wheel. That's the Australia I know.

For me, it's not only the ethical or moral or even the spiritual element of doing good that makes changing people's lives meaningful. There's something inherently good about helping to improve someone's life. Helping a person who's really struggling, enabling them to take control of their life and make decisions about their future and their family's future– that's what it's about. A lot of people 'get' doing good. But for many of those people, the act of doing good is not so much about helping someone else; it's about doing something for themselves. They do it because it makes them feel good; by doing something for someone else, they get something back in return. Hence the name Good Return! I think that's okay.

Truthfully, what I've done has been good for me, too. People say to me, 'You're doing such good work for others,' but ultimately, it's for myself. I've done what I have because I believed in it. And because it was meaningful to other people, and benefitted other people, it was meaningful to me. I must admit I also did it because it was new and different and exciting. Whether the act of doing good is selfless or not, it's worth doing it in a way that empirical evidence has shown is doing good. That's what makes it meaningful for me: having proof that you're doing good. That's why I spend a lot of time explaining the rational argument. If I'm going to choose between different good acts, then I'll choose one that I know will have the biggest impact.

That's why I choose microfinance, because I believe the act of doing good in microfinance gives a bigger bang – not just for the buck, but for the time that I'm investing in that particular activity – rather than in other forms of aid. And yes, I admit that I do get something out of it, knowing I'm doing good. I get a sense of achievement; I get a sense of having made a difference. I feel that I'm leaving a legacy. There's many reasons – moral, ethical, emotional, economic – why the act of helping others is good. But my choice to help others through microfinance is completely rational.

This argument around the rationality of microfinance is one of the pitches that I use when I talk to people. I believe it's helped bring in a lot of volunteers, including some very senior business people. A lot of people in Australia raise money for charity. I don't want to be cynical, but people's choice of which charity to donate to has a lot to do with which ones have the best publicity and marketing strategies. It's not usually a rational choice. People don't generally weigh up the evidence on how and where their dollar will have the most impact.

But people are generous, on the whole. Of course, in my fundraising, I've made a point of trying to get to know the wealthy, especially in Sydney. They obviously have more money to give. Some are very generous, but others…

I remember one woman. I asked her if she could support our work. She said no, she couldn't afford to support Good Return. She and her husband were really struggling to buy the house they wanted, a

$5-million house overlooking the water. She said it was really hard for her; all her friends had houses worth at least $7 million or $8 million, but it was a real stretch for her to manage $5 million, so they really couldn't afford to give to us. Well…that's okay. People make choices.

And then I think of the people who have been incredibly generous. Neild McIntosh's parents, for example. Neild's father, David, is an amazing guy. He started Austral Refrigeration, which became part of a public company. When I first met him and his wife Colleen, they must've been in their early seventies. They lived south of the airport, in Botany Bay: nice house, double-storey, on the water. Anyway, their neighbour, who was in her eighties, apparently had some problem with her roof or gutter. David said to her, 'Paying a plumber is ridiculous. I'll fix it for you!' So he got out his ladder and up he went and fixed the gutter himself – and this is a guy in his seventies! He could've paid ten plumbers, if he'd wanted to! That same year, he and Colleen made a very large donation to Good Return, and they gave a similar amount to about ten other charities. They just want to share what they have. He lives fairly simply and his success hasn't changed him. He told me once, 'I was just lucky: I was in the right place at the right time.' An amazingly humble guy. He and Colleen have been the biggest individual donors to Good Return. I just take my hat off to them. And then there's the story of that woman struggling to buy her $5-million waterfront house. As I said, we all make choices.

There's a case study that's used in business school to demonstrate good management practice. The case study focuses on a CEO who instigated a 360-degree review of his own performance. He asked his peers, his staff, and his board to give him their honest assessment of him. In terms of his ability to achieve results, the results were predictably good; the CEO was well respected for his business acumen. But in terms of his personal attributes, it was a different story. His staff and his peers saw him as a harsh taskmaster who didn't care about people's well-being – their health, or their family situation. The CEO was really shocked. He made a deliberate decision to change and he turned his life around. He became a Buddhist and meditated regularly. That CEO was Gordon Cairns, our board member: another very generous man and my close personal friend.

∞

I'm not particularly religious. As I said before, I consider myself an agnostic Christian – a 'Chagnostic', as Brontë once put it! Technically, you're a Christian if you believe in Christ: it's about what you believe, not what you do. I don't subscribe to that. I think of Christianity with a small 'c', defined by how you live your life and how you give back to your family and your community. I believe in Christianity in terms of action: doing good, being the good Samaritan – the behaviour, that's what I believe is important.

For the last year I've been on the board of the Salvation Army. I'm also on the board of Habitat for Humanity, which is also a faith-based organisation – a Christian organisation – but you don't have to be a Christian to be accepted there. I really like the fact that they're inclusive; not all faith-based organisations are like that. A lot of the international aid agencies in Australia are faith-based.

I remember once attending a function held by the Australian Council for International Development, the umbrella organisation for Australian NGOs, with a friend of mine, Clay O'Brien.

This guy came up to us and said, 'Hey, you two! You're doing great work. You guys are real Christians!'

Clay responded first and said, 'Yes!', which came as a bit of a surprise. I never knew that he was a Christian.

This guy then asked him, 'What church do you go to?', and Clay answered, 'Church of England.'

Well, this guy clearly wasn't impressed. He just said, 'Oh!' What he implied was that Church of England doesn't really count, so you're not a real Christian. It turned out that he was with the Hill Song group.

I don't want to judge anyone, but I do feel judged sometimes. The spiritual values I believe in are inclusive, not judgemental.

Christians assert there's only one God, and I guess I'm a complete heretic by saying I'm not a hundred per cent sure of that. In that sense, I'm not a Christian. I really admire the Buddhist faith. My friend Gordon is a committed Buddhist, and I respect and admire him. He never explicitly refers to his beliefs, but he represents those beliefs and values in the way he behaves, the way he engages with people. That appeals to me in terms of faith: practising, not preaching what you believe.

If there is a God, I like to think of her as female, a kind of Mother Earth. God seems to be more female than male. I like the idea of there being a God who is good and who believes in good triumphing over evil. Jacqui says I look up in the sky and see a set of scales. Maybe choosing good over evil is just part of what's in ourselves. Maybe the best part of ourselves is God.

I have to confess that when I got this diagnosis and prognosis, I thought God had lost my file in the move to computerisation! I don't know if turning to one's spiritual beliefs or looking for some spiritual entity is part of this journey of reflection that I'm on now. It may well be. I can't always articulate this well, but having someone, or something, to pray to and to rail against is important to me now. I don't think anyone else wants to hear or should have to put up with the anger and the resentment and the fear and the hurt that you feel when you've been told that you've got limited time left. God is like a split personality within me that I talk to and shout at. Maybe that's all it is.

∞

If I've only got limited time left, I want to live it as well as I can. In a way, the cancer is my final test of the quality of my life. How well one has lived one's life shows when things are challenging, not when things are easy. It reminds me of John F. Kennedy's moon speech. 'We choose to go to the moon in this decade and do other things,' he said, 'not because they are easy, but because they are hard.'

∞

Good Return was the child I gave birth to; it's a mature adult now. It's bigger than me. It's been bigger than me for a while. It's a community organisation: it's the staff, the board, the volunteers, and our partner microfinance institutions. But it's more than that, too – more than the sum of its parts.

In the last couple of years, we started looking at potential mergers between Good Return and other organisations. This was a logical step if we were to ensure our future security and continue to grow. But of course a merger brings risks. We've made a huge investment – we, our partners, and our investors and donors – in time and energy and effort into building a values-based organisation. I'm not worried about the potential loss of my legacy, but I would hate to see the organisation changing from one that is driven by its values to one that is driven purely by profit. The other thing that I'd be worried about losing is the value we place on our volunteers. If we were to merge with another organisation, volunteers might not be as welcomed. They might not be so valued or respected. They wouldn't engage as much. That's what I worry about: losing whatever this thing is that the volunteers have come to love, and the staff have come to love, and we've come to recognise as unique. I'd worry about losing that.

∞

On one of my trips to the Philippines a few years ago, I was due to visit a number of savings and loans groups. I travelled out to the barangays – the villages – accompanied by the field officer and a staff member from the partner microfinance organisation. One particular morning we were to meet a women's savings and loans group that had been going for a few years. When we arrived in the barangay, no one had gathered yet. That's not unusual; people have their own lives to get on with and they can't afford to wait around for a meeting that may or may not happen, so sometimes we'd need to wait for people to assemble.

On this occasion, we were waiting by the road outside the barangay captain's house and we saw a woman working in her field about a hundred metres away. The field officer with us called to her, and she looked up. We waved, and she waved back and started walking across the field towards us. I reached out my hand to shake hers; she was a bit reluctant at first, because her hands were dirty from working in the field, but I assured her it didn't matter. She laughed, wiped her hands on her skirt, took my hand briefly and we got talking. She had some English, as many people do in the Philippines, so we could talk to each other with a little bit of support from the staff of our partner organisation. She invited us to her house, and we followed her there. The house was small, simple and basic: really just a small thatched timber hut. We went inside and sat together on a wooden bench. There was very little furniture; just a table and a bench and a picture of Christ on the wall, probably cut out of a magazine. The bed mats were rolled neatly and stacked in one corner. She offered me a drink and then we talked. She told me how the loans and the savings services had enabled her to overcome economic shocks. She didn't express it in those words, of course, but basically what she was saying was that when the price of produce went down – like the price of tomatoes, say, or mangoes – she could then rely on her savings or she could take out a loan to carry her through until the price went back up again. Incredibly, she and her husband had saved enough to send her daughter to college, and her daughter had won a scholarship to go to university.

I hope I didn't show it, but that woman's story brought tears to my eyes. I felt humbled by how my small contribution through the work of Good Return was helping this woman, and hundreds, if not thousands of women like her. Her aspirations for herself were very modest, or perhaps I should say realistic. But her aspirations for her daughter – to go to university! Even now, recalling this story, I have tears in my eye.

Sometime later, I heard from the CEO of our partner organisation in the Philippines that the daughter of that woman had completed her degree and was now working at that very same organisation, our partner financial institution. She was now helping to provide savings and loans services to women like her mother. That's just one story.

That was just one woman. There are dozens more stories like that. By helping one woman, you're helping her family and you're helping her community. You're not just helping one woman, you're helping thousands of women – literally hundreds of thousands. And by helping them, you're helping their families. You're helping the next generation. To date, Good Return has improved the lives – either directly or indirectly – of more than six hundred thousand women. I'm really proud of that. The rationalist in me says helping one woman is great, but helping six hundred thousand women is fantastic!

∞

My mother used to say that life is like a book: it has a beginning, a middle and an end. This reflected her attitude to life: live for today, accept whatever happens, and keep on going. See humour wherever it can be found. Be grateful for whatever unexpected joys you find in your book of life…

In her acceptance of life and all it brings – the joys and sorrows, the expected and the unexpected – my mother lived each day as she found it, with kindness and without regret. Ultimately, my mother believed there are only two ways to live your life. One is as though nothing is a miracle. The other is as though everything is a miracle.

# Afterword

After Guy announced his retirement as CEO of Good Return in 2016, a gala fundraising event was held in his honour at The Establishment in George Street, in Sydney's CBD, attended by more than two hundred people.

Gordon Cairns stood up and made a speech.

Ladies and Gentlemen, it is my privilege tonight to pay special thanks to Guy Winship, and to honour him.

I have known Guy for nearly ten years and am proud to call him a friend. For those who may not know him as well, let me share with you his impressive career.

Relocating to Australia in 2002 with his family, he founded what is now Good Return in his study, using his own money as seed funding. The organisation doubled in size in 2003, when Shane joined. Now we have sixty-two staff, eight ambassadors and ten directors. In 2004 our annual income was $159,000. Last year it was over $3 million. We have over five thousand supporters, including distinguished corporates such as Accenture, Westpac, Clayton Utz, Deloitte and Origin Energy.

But most importantly, through his tireless efforts we have funded over nine thousand direct loans, with the average loan size of $350, and a repayment rate of 99.99 per cent. We have trained over forty thousand families across Asia Pacific and reached over six hundred thousand people. This is a truly remarkable achievement, and a wonderful legacy that Guy leaves.

But Guy is more than the consummate professional and microfinance expert. He is a gentle man. He has dedicated his life, from early days in South Africa, to drive for social justice and more recently to eliminate poverty. It is a noble purpose, which has inspired those around him. He is a modest man, always crediting the team with the remarkable achievements. He is a courageous man, confronting his mortality with humour and stoicism. Who can forget his response to losing one eye to cancer – that one-eyed managers made faster decisions, and that only his squash would suffer as a result!

And so tonight I want to pay special thanks to Guy, and to Jacqui his wife, and their children. None of us know what the future may hold for us. For them, may they have a special place in our thoughts and prayers. For Guy is a special man. His legacy is remarkable, and we owe it to him to build on it. But as a gentleman he has inspired those around him and we are the better for knowing him.

Gordon then turned to Guy and embraced him, and he wept.

*Guy and Jacqui, Church Point, Sydney, April 2015.*

# Acknowledgements

My greatest debt of gratitude is to Guy himself. If it wasn't for his trust in me and his enthusiasm for the idea of writing the story of his life, this book would never have been started. And if it wasn't for his ongoing commitment and courage in the face of the bully, it would never have been finished.

Warmest thanks to Jacqui Winship for her support throughout. Her careful editing and augmentation of the final manuscript are deeply appreciated. Many thanks too to Guy's and Jacqui's friends Stephen Matthews and Lyndsay Brown for their contributions.

I am especially grateful to Melodie Buendia for transcribing many hours of recorded conversations, and to Virginia Lloyd for her insightful editing and valuable comments on the first complete draft.

Heartfelt thanks to family and friends for their support and encouragement. In particular, special thanks to my daughter, Annie O'Connell, for her sharp eyes, clever questions and helpful suggestions, and to my dearest friend, Rosemary Knight, for her honest and constructive feedback on an early draft. And to all of you, thank you for believing I could do this.

Finally, endless thanks to my wonderful husband, Martin Nightingale, for his love, patience, understanding and unwavering support – and for his inspired ideas on how to breathe life into the story.

Sally Rynveld, January 2018

www.ingramcontent.com/pod-product-compliance
Lightning Source LLC
Chambersburg PA
CBHW071822080526
44589CB00012B/884